Breaking The Yoke
Of Spiritual Oppression

by Dale Anderson

Scripture quotations in this book are taken from the King
James Version of the *Holy Bible*.

All definitions in this book are taken from *Webster's Ninth
New Collegiate Dictionary* unless otherwise indicated.

Printed in the United States of America.
ISBN 1-888251-35-2

Cover design by Marshall Jones, Voppa.com

To order *Breaking The Yoke Of Spiritual Oppression*
Go to: www.daystarpublications.com

You may contact the author via email at:
danderson@daystarpublications.com

Acknowledgments

I am very grateful to Leslie Rosier for her invaluable support, excellent suggestions and untiring efforts throughout the last four years. I also want to express my appreciation to Laurel Gleeson for her part in editing the final manuscript and for being willing to meet the deadlines. And, I wish to express a heartfelt thanks to all of my family and friends who endured, without complaint, both my conversations about the book and their reading of the chapters for content and clarity.

I give special honor to my pastor, Reverend Paul Mooney, first and foremost for his godly example and for the love and compassion he has extended to my family. And, secondly, I want to thank him for his insightful suggestions regarding the manuscript and to acknowledge that the final product was much improved by his efforts.

I sincerely appreciate Reverend Nathaniel Haney for his willingness to read this book two times: initially in the early stages of writing and a second time when the manuscript was completed. His encouragement and support helped me to believe that the task could be accomplished.

I also want to thank Reverend Jerry Ensey for his suggestions and assistance in several of the final stages of publishing the book.

A special thanks to Marshall Jones for his expertise in designing the cover.

Dedicated to my children—Dianne, Joshua, Amber and Andrew

Dianne, who enabled me to understand "grace and glory"
Joshua, who was given as "the blessing"
Amber, whose life has enabled me to "believe in miracles"
Andrew, who became my "valley of deliverance"

Thank you for your love

Contents

Introduction

Awaking in the early morning hours as daybreak began to extinguish the darkness of night, I glanced at a picture hanging on the wall opposite my bed. A little eight-year-old girl with soft golden-brown curls and laughing bright blue eyes stared back at me. Her cheerful and serene countenance gave the impression that she possessed not only a carefree spirit, but also a passion for life. I pondered whether her spirit still resided within me, if so, I would be anticipating the fulfillment of dreams and visions yet to be experienced in life. Surely, hopelessness could not coexist with her childlike faith. I desperately wanted to connect with the spirit of the little girl in the picture and know who I was at that time and who I would have become if the light of her spirit had not been quenched. Would I ever be reunited with her spirit or was that part of me choked out, never to live again? While still pondering these thoughts, I rose to begin another day, anticipating that this day would be like all the other days in the last six years that were filled with despondency and despair. Life had become a maze, the passages of which gradually but steadily grew darker and more confusing resulting in a groping kind of existence. The further I journeyed, the more isolated I became. Bewilderment, hopelessness and despair were my constant companions. Each night brought only the dread of facing another day. Could there be a way of escape from this emotionally crippled state or would I continue this desolate journey until death?

David of Old had likewise journeyed down a path of desolation and despair. He, however, found a way of escape when he cried unto the Lord:

> Give ear to my prayer, O God; and hide not thyself from my supplication. Attend unto me, and hear me: I mourn in my complaint, and make a noise; Because of the voice of the enemy, because of the oppression of the wicked: for they cast iniquity upon me, and in wrath they hate me. My heart is sore pained within me: and the terrors of death are fallen upon me. Fearfulness and trembling are come upon me, and horror hath overwhelmed me. And I said, Oh that I had wings like a dove! for then would I fly away, and be at rest. Lo, then would I wander far off, and remain in the wilderness. Selah. I would hasten my escape from the windy storm and tempest . . . As for me, I will call upon God; and the Lord shall save me. Evening, and morning, and at noon, will I pray, and cry aloud: and he shall hear my voice. He hath delivered my soul in peace from the battle that was against me . . . Cast thy burden upon the Lord, and he shall sustain thee: he shall never suffer the righteous to be moved. (Psalm 55:1-8; 16-17; 22)

> Thou tellest my wanderings: put thou my tears into thy bottle: are they not in thy book? When I cry unto thee, then shall mine

enemies turn back: this I know; for God is for me. In God will I praise his word: in the Lord will I praise his word. In God have I put my trust: I will not be afraid what man can do unto me. Thy vows are upon me, O God: I will render praises unto thee. For thou hast delivered my soul from death: wilt not thou deliver my feet from falling, that I may walk before God in the light of the living?
(Psalm 56:8-13)

This book is my testimony of how God came to me in a place of emotional and spiritual desolation, and taking me by the hand, gently led me out of the darkness into His glorious light. Patiently, He taught me how to live victoriously over the battles raging in my mind and through the storms surrounding my life. My desire is that every person reading this book will receive the healing and deliverance that God will bestow on those who call upon Him. And, secondly, that this book will serve as a resource for those who are ministering to individuals who are in need of spiritual or emotional healing and deliverance.

Part One

Breaking the Yoke of Spiritual Oppression

Is not this the fast that I have chosen? to loose the bands of wickedness, to undo the heavy burdens, and to let the oppressed go free, and that ye break every yoke? (Isaiah 58:6)

In righteousness shalt thou be established: thou shalt be far from oppression; for thou shalt not fear: and from terror; for it shall not come near thee. (Isaiah 54:14)

And it shall come to pass in that day, that his burden shall be taken away from off thy shoulder, and his yoke from off thy neck, and the yoke shall be destroyed because of the anointing. (Isaiah 10:27)

Chapter One

Wilt Thou be Made Whole?

God in His infinite wisdom and compassion has made provision for the healing and deliverance of individuals who are emotionally crippled. Before addressing God's plan and promises, it is necessary to understand what is meant by the term "emotionally crippled."

While writing this book, the word "crippled" repeatedly came to mind as an accurate description of the emotional plight of individuals for whom this book was written. The word "crippled" is defined as "to deprive of strength, efficiency, wholeness, or capability for service." Although this definition seems more applicable when referring to a physical disability, the definition is equally appropriate when describing a state of emotional disability. Emotional crippling is as tangible as physical crippling, though it may not be as perceptible. Emotional instability overshadows every area of an individual's life, not only in the natural but also in the spiritual.

Physical and emotional disabilities vary in severity. A person may have a crippled hand or a crippled leg and there are even those who have lost the use of all four extremities. Likewise, there are varying degrees of emotional crippling. An individual who has experienced severe emotional trauma over an extended period of time may be as debilitated as a person who is totally paralyzed.

The "good news" is that the severity of the emotional crippling does not alter the effectiveness of the remedy that God has provided. No matter how severe an individual's emotional problems may be, God's plan is sufficient. His plan is to **Restore**, **Renew** and **Revive** that individual mentally, emotionally, physically and spiritually. Jesus poses this question to all who suffer from mental or emotional afflictions: "Wilt thou be made whole?" (John 5:6).

Restoration

From Genesis to Revelation, the Scriptures declare God's restorative power. David cried to the Lord, "Restore unto me the joy of thy salvation . . ." (Psalm 51:12). A man with a withered hand was restored whole at the command of Jesus (Mark 3:1-5). A blind man's sight was restored after Jesus touched him (Mark 8:22-25). The act of restoration means to bring back to a former, unimpaired state or condition. The miracle of restoration is not limited to only the physical or spiritual realm but extends also to the mind and emotions of man.

The gospels of Luke and Mark each give an account of the man from the country of the Gadarenes, who Jesus restored to his "right mind." Prior to this man's restoration, the scriptures portrayed his emotionally and spiritually oppressed state as well as his self-destructive behaviors:

> And when he went forth to land, there met
> him out of the city a certain man, which had

devils long time, and ware no clothes, neither abode in any house, but in the tombs.
 (Luke 8:27)

Who had his dwelling among the tombs; and no man could bind him, no, not with chains: Because that he had been often bound with fetters and chains, and the chains had been plucked asunder by him, and the fetters broken in pieces: neither could any man tame him. And always, night and day, he was in the mountains, and in the tombs, crying, and cutting himself with stones. (Mark 5:3-5)

If this same man lived in the present time he would, no doubt, be admitted to the psychiatric unit of a hospital and started on one or more psychotropic (mind/mood-altering) medications. The medications may subdue his aggressive and self-destructive behaviors, but they would not alleviate the torment in his mind. Jesus, however, had knowledge of this man's physical, mental and spiritual state before He ever encountered him. He knew that the man needed more than to have just his behavior subdued and his physical wounds healed; he also needed deliverance from the spiritual oppression that plagued him. After Jesus cast the demons out of the man, the people in the city and in the country went out to see what was done:

[They] came to Jesus, and found the man, out of whom the devils were departed, sitting at the feet of Jesus, clothed, and in his *right mind*: and they were afraid. (Luke 8:35) (Italics mine)

5

We are not told the life story of this man or what terrible circumstances had befallen him that led to his pitiful mental and spiritual state. With Jesus, neither the cause nor the severity of the emotional affliction matters. It only matters that a person recognizes that Jesus has provided a remedy for his crippled state and that if he will turn to Jesus, he can be restored to his right mind.

One might think this is not an appropriate example, presuming that emotional problems have little to do with spiritual oppression or demon possession. However, within the dynamics of every emotional problem there exists a spiritual aspect as *all men* are influenced by the spirit world. Whether an individual recognizes this truth may directly influence his decision regarding the source of the remedy for his emotional or mental problem. For a Christian, the spiritual aspect of emotional problems must always be considered. The Bible declares that we have an adversary, the devil, who, ". . . as a roaring lion, walketh about, seeking whom he may devour" (I Peter 5:8).

The above account of the deliverance and healing of the man from Gadara is an excellent example of the Lord's ability to restore an individual's mental health and emotional stability. Even when the cause of a mental problem is the result of the worst possible source—demon possession—this is not to be considered even a slight hindrance for our God. Whether through healing and/or deliverance, God is able to *completely restore* an individual's mental and emotional state to a former, unimpaired condition.

Certain individuals, however, cannot even remember ever being mentally unimpaired, as the neglect or abuse they suffered began while they were an infant or a small child. The question may be asked then, to what unimpaired state would they be restored? God knew these individuals when they were yet in the womb and likewise, knew what they would have been like had they not been emotionally scarred from infancy or childhood. Through Christ they are able to experience restoration, transformation and regeneration as ". . . old things are passed away [and] . . .all things are become new" (II Corinthians 5:17).

Renewal

Among other physical maladies, emotionally crippled people commonly experience a disruption in their normal sleep patterns. Some individuals sleep a good part of the day yet never feel rested. Others may have extended periods of insomnia leaving them drained physically and mentally. Since sleep is crucial to the renewing of both physical and mental strength, these people continually feel exhausted, which in turn contributes to their increased emotional instability.

The mental fatigue associated with emotional instability often deprives individuals of their normal ability to process their thoughts effectively. Subsequent mental activities conducive to a productive and self-sufficient lifestyle are impaired. An inability to focus, frequently accompanied by mental distraction, results in difficulty making decisions, drawing conclusions or carrying out decisive actions. Maintaining full-time or even part-time employment may become difficult, if not impossible.

Emotionally crippled people who have experienced long-term stress usually have multiple physiological conditions involving any or all of the body systems. Gastrointestinal symptoms are common and are usually intensified by poor eating habits. During one extended period of emotional instability that I went through, I experienced at times a tendency to over-eat, and at other times a lack of appetite. Usually, I felt like over-eating for two reasons. Primarily, eating was one of the only activities that was accompanied by a feeling of pleasure. Secondly, since I felt exhausted continually, eating seemed an appropriate solution to that problem, but it created another problem—that of gaining unwanted pounds. At times, however, I experienced a lack of appetite and subsequent weight loss.

Another physiological symptom associated with emotional instability is frequent headaches. Some individuals have a headache on a daily basis varying in intensity from mild to severe. Migraine headaches intense enough to cause people to be bedridden are not uncommon.

A correlation also exists between emotional problems and a depleted immune system, causing an individual to be susceptible to disease. With the passing of time, emotionally crippled people will continue to deteriorate both mentally and physically. The cumulative effect of their physical, emotional and spiritual decline results in a feeling of utter helplessness, which in turn progresses to a state of hopelessness. Without renewed mental, physical and spiritual strength, even a Christian may be tempted to surrender in the spiritual battle raging against him.

Jesus is able to renew a Christian's mental, physical and spiritual strength. David in Psalm 103:1-5 wrote about many of the benefits that are available to those who serve the Lord:

> Bless the Lord, O my soul: and all that is within me, bless his holy name. Bless the

Lord, O my soul, and forget not all his benefits: Who forgiveth all thine iniquities; who healeth all thy diseases; Who redeemeth thy life from destruction; who crowneth thee with lovingkindness and tender mercies; Who satisfieth thy mouth with good things; so that thy *youth is renewed like the eagle's*. (Italics mine)

Of particular interest in these scriptures are the words "renew" and "youth." There are several definitions associated with the word "renew:" "to make like new: restore to freshness, vigor, or perfection . . . to make new spiritually: regenerate . . . to restore to existence: revive [and]. . . to restore lost strength." The preceding scriptures portray the benefits that God has provided for His children enabling them to experience renewed mental and physical strength even to the degree that they possessed in their youth.

There have been two periods of time during my life when I have experienced severe spiritual oppression. The initial episode occurred while in my thirties and lasted for approximately six years. The second episode, which took place about three years later, lasted only eight months. During both episodes, I experienced a decline in my mental, physical and spiritual strength. The following testimony relating the details of my second experience with emotional oppression demonstrates the power of God to heal, deliver and renew a Christian's strength.

Shortly after I began to increase the time I was spending in prayer each day, I noticed a gradual change in my emotions. Often, I felt sad and in addition to the sadness, I noticed that I became easily fatigued. Over the course of several months I grew progressively weaker and more emotional. Dedicating more time to prayer would seemingly shield a person from the spiritual attack of the adversary; however, Satan intensifies his efforts to deter prayer because he fears a Christian's prayers. He knows that prayer is a threat to his domain of darkness.

I was not consciously aware of the degree of the spiritual attack being waged against me and attributed the increasing weariness and emotional instability to being overwhelmed by my responsibilities as a single parent. As the months passed, I could no longer deny that I had fallen prey to the influence of an oppressive spirit of depression.

One day, a friend called to invite me to visit her and attend a conference being held at her church. She lived in another state approximately eight hours away. While en route to the conference, I experienced an intense spiritual attack. Plagued with feelings of fear and anxiety, I debated whether or not I could continue the trip, but after praying, I decided that I would not turn back. In addition to having a pounding headache, I felt nauseated and exhausted.

Arriving later than expected at my friend's apartment, we agreed that she would go ahead to church and that I would meet her there. While getting ready for church I became increasingly apprehensive and felt tormented by thoughts of not wanting to be with people because of the discouragement I felt. I had difficulty deciding what to wear as none of the outfits I tried on, in my opinion, looked good on me. My frustration mounted as I realized that I would be late and attract attention to myself when I walked into the church. Amidst all the roaring of the demonic forces, I heard a still small voice inside of me telling me to go to the church anyway.

A consistent habit of church attendance undergirded my

resolve to go to church that night, though I continued to struggle with my tormented thoughts and emotions. Though the demonic spirits that accompanied me to church were invisible, I was acutely aware of the battle that raged in my mind as I got out of the car and walked toward the door of the church. From the spirit of darkness there came a distinct impression into my mind: *You will feel the same way when you come out of there, only you will have made a fool of yourself.* Resisting this thought, I continued toward the church.

I feared that some of the people in the church would be able to perceive my oppressed state of mind. I especially feared the discernment of the evangelist and tried to be as inconspicuous as possible, making my way quickly to a seat near the back of the sanctuary.

The message being preached was, of course, exactly what I needed to hear. The evangelist, Reverend Lee Stoneking, was preaching about deliverance. He explained that as children of God we do not need to yield to the influence of the devil who is attempting to oppress our minds. He further described how an individual could discern the difference between oppression and possession. Oppression, he explained, is when someone feels as though a force is weighing down upon him and the pressure is from the outside. Possession, on the other hand, is when a person feels the force or pressure coming from within himself. The oppression I was feeling was an outside force and was so intense that I did not want to wait for the end of the service for my deliverance. The Lord conveniently arranged for a mid-service deliverance so I could enjoy the rest of the message and the service. About halfway through his message, Brother Stoneking asked for those who needed deliverance to stand. He then gave step-by-step directions as to what to think and say to the devil. The instructions were very simple. He said, *"Envision your mind as having a window. Open the window and tell the devil to get out! Since he is an uninvited guest, he has no right to be there, and we have the right to tell him to get out!"* Immediately, after commanding the oppressive spirit to leave, the evil spirit was gone, as were my headache, nausea and physical exhaustion. I was healed and delivered and a renewed strength surged through my body.

Though the devil was not physically inside of my mind, he was exerting an oppressive force against my mind. The yoke of spiritual oppression was broken when I commanded the evil spirit to leave. As God's children, we have the power to overcome the evil one. The anointing of His Spirit will destroy every yoke of bondage because "Christ hath made us free" (Galatians 5:1).

The most wonderful part of God's healing and deliverance is that the whole process takes only a matter of seconds. No long sessions of introspective thinking or counseling were needed to determine the cause and events that led me to this state. No assessment of who may or may not be to blame for my emotional problems, no ongoing therapy sessions—just quick and easy deliverance.

For the "doubting Thomas" readers, of whom I might once have been one, skepticism will quickly pose this question: *Did the demon of depression try to overcome her after that?* Of course! The demonic spirit did attempt to overpower me again. The devil always makes a series of rebound plays.

Approximately one week after my deliverance and healing, during a time of prayer, I became aware of a presence that was overshadowing me. Like an invisible cloud, the darkness surrounded me and I began to feel fear.

I said to the Lord, *"Oh no, it's here again, and there is no Brother Stoneking or conference going on."* An impression instantly came to my mind in response to my plea: *Do you think it takes Brother Stoneking and a conference to be delivered again? Tell him to get out!* So I did, and the result was the same—he left. I have commanded the spirit of darkness to depart many times since that experience. The remedy is simple, yet powerful! Resisting and commanding Satan to leave is one of the spiritual weapons available to a Christian to overcome the spirit of darkness and to break the yoke of oppression.

Another aspect of spiritual oppression Christians need to be cognizant of is that Satan will try not only to oppress them with thoughts of hopelessness and despair, but he will also accuse them of being a failure in their walk with God. Spiritual oppression is often accompanied by a feeling of reproach in response to either one's own judgment of himself or sometimes the judgment of others who presume the oppressed individual is tampering with sin or is negligent in his consecration to God.

Prior to and during this eight-month episode of spiritual oppression, I maintained a daily prayer life. I was actively involved in teaching Bible studies and in youth work. The week just prior to the special services mentioned in the preceding paragraphs, I had been fasting in an attempt to overcome the oppression I was experiencing. In retrospect, the only thing I can honestly say that the Lord was dealing with me about, before or after my deliverance, was His will for me to write this book.

For several reasons I had been reluctant to attempt to write this book, though I was fully convinced that the Lord was leading me to this endeavor. I lacked self-confidence and did not think that I had the ability to write a book.

Also, I did not want to relive any of the memories of the first episode of spiritual oppression that I had endured for six years. In spite of my fears and reservations, after experiencing God's deliverance and healing, I was willing and obedient and began writing. The experience had rekindled an acute awareness of the mental and emotional agony that accompanies spiritual oppression. I also felt a renewed appreciation for the blessing of receiving God's healing and deliverance and His ability to renew a person's mental, physical and spiritual strength.

Emotional/Spiritual Revival

People suffering from long-term emotional despair exist in a state which could be compared to *"living death."* Their countenances reveal the hopelessness, gloom and oppression they are experiencing. These individuals often wish to die and may even pray to die. They are vulnerable to a spirit of suicide.

Near the end of my first episode of spiritual oppression, which as stated previously lasted for six years, I began to seriously contemplate suicide. The demonic spirits of depression and suicide are usually inseparable companions. Since I felt more dead than alive, what would it matter if I died? I had neither a fear of death nor a desire to live. However, I had a great fear of being lost and, therefore, would make no attempt to end my life. This God-given fear—a fear that can be stifled by the influence of pyschotropic drugs—preserved my life. (This subject will be discussed in greater detail in a later chapter.)

During those agonizing years, I rarely noticed the sunshine, trees or anything pleasant in my surroundings. And, even though there were many good things in my life, I was unable to enjoy those things. I did not want to go to sleep at night because I did not want to wake up the next morning and live through another day of hopelessness and despair. Thank God for His love and faithfulness. He will not leave His children in a state of hopelessness, but will revive them in the midst of their trouble:

> Though I walk in the midst of trouble, thou wilt *revive* me: thou shalt stretch forth thine hand against the wrath of mine enemies, and thy right hand shall save me. The Lord will perfect that which concerneth me: thy mercy, O Lord, endureth forever: forsake not the works of thine own hands. (Psalm 138:7-8) (Italics mine)

> For thus saith the high and lofty One that inhabiteth eternity, whose name is Holy; I dwell in the high and holy place, with him also that is of a contrite and humble spirit, to *revive* the spirit of the humble, and to *revive* the heart of the contrite ones. (Isaiah 57:15) (Italics mine)

The word "revive" is defined as "to restore to consciousness or life . . . to restore from a depressed, inactive, or unused state . . . to renew in the mind or memory." "Revive" comes from the Latin word "revivere," which means "to live again." God is able to revive His child mentally, physically and spiritually to a place of feeling alive and well, and to give him a renewed awareness of the good things in life. The miracle of being revived creates not only a desire to live but also a passion for life.

"Inexplicable joy" would even fall short of describing how I felt when I was delivered from the spiritual oppression I experienced during those years. To understand the renewed joy of "feeling alive," one would need to have some concept of the hopelessness I endured. Over the years, walls were erected in my mind in a feeble attempt to shield and protect myself from the circumstances to which I was exposed. The walls that were meant to protect me became my prison. Both the self-imposed confinement and the darkness of my thoughts intensified the confusion, hopelessness and despair I felt. Escape from this prison, by any means, seemed impossible. During those years, I never knew if I would ever feel alive again or would even want to live again. Joy and happiness even to the slightest degree eluded me.

As I cried to God from that place of torment, He heard my cry and delivered me. The walls of the prison were demolished, the demon of depression was vanquished and I was set free from that pit of despair. I was alive! Free to laugh and play with my children again and to be aware of the touch of their cheeks against mine as I hugged them. I had a renewed consciousness of the warmth of the sun, the blue sky and the sound of birds singing in the trees. I was aware of all the sights and sounds I had been surrounded with every day of those six years but had been unable to experience or enjoy. Strength flowed through my body, causing me to feel as if I could run through a troop and leap over a wall. My feet truly had been set on the high places (Psalm 18:29-35). There are several passages in this same chapter of Psalms in which the psalmist described the deliverance afforded those who call upon the Lord:

I will call upon the Lord, who is worthy to be praised: so shall I be saved from mine enemies. The sorrows of death compassed me, and the floods of ungodly men made me afraid. The sorrows of hell compassed me about: the snares of death prevented me. In my distress I called upon the Lord, and cried unto my God: he heard my voice out of his temple, and my cry came before him, even into his ears. (Psalm 18:3-6)

He sent from above, he took me, he drew me out of many waters. He delivered me from my strong enemy, and from them which hated me: for they were too strong for me. They prevented me in the day of my calamity: but the Lord was my stay. He brought me forth also into a large place; he delivered me, because he delighted in me. (Psalm 18:16-19)

For thou wilt light my candle: the Lord my God will enlighten my darkness. (Psalm 18:28)

The only stipulation that must be met for a person to experience God's deliverance is that he must call upon the Lord. If there is sin in an individual's life, then God will grant him the knowledge of repentance, as sin is usually the avenue by which demonic forces oppress an individual. Though the storms of life may come, God has made provision for His body, the church, to enjoy not only a life of righteousness but also to experience peace and joy. "For the kingdom of God is not meat and drink; but righteousness, and peace, and joy in the Holy Ghost" (Romans 14:17).

The peace and joy that God gives, however, is not predicated upon a life free of trials and suffering. The fifth chapter of Matthew recorded Jesus teaching about some of the trials that a Christian may endure. Jesus said,

> But I say unto you, Love your enemies, bless them that curse you, do good to them that hate you, and pray for them which despitefully use you, and persecute you; That ye may be the children of your Father which is in heaven: for he maketh his sun to rise on the evil and on the good, and sendeth rain on the just and on the unjust. (44-45)

As explained in the preceding verses, all people, whether just or unjust, will face the storms of life and attacks of the adversary, but a Christian has God as his source of help. And, though there are some circumstances in life that may cause Christians to experience a brief absence of the peace and joy that God has promised them, when they cry out to Him during those times of emotional suffering, He will restore, renew and revive them.

Chapter Two

Bible Philosophy

One of the greatest challenges Christians face is to maintain a scriptural philosophy of life in a time when there are many anti-Christian philosophies making inroads into our American culture. Of these philosophies, none is so pervasive as the doctrine of humanism, the tentacles of which have reached into every part of our society.

Secular Humanism

Humanism is defined as, "a doctrine, attitude, or way of life centered on human interests or values; a philosophy that usually rejects supernaturalism and stresses an individual's dignity, worth, and capacity for self-realization through reason" Secularism is defined as an "indifference to or rejection or exclusion of religion and religious considerations." Secular humanism, a philosophy derived from humanism and a growing sentiment of indifference to or rejection of religious considerations about life, is the foundation for the predominant trend of thinking in America today. As a consequence of this philosophy infiltrating our society particularly in the arenas of education, government, social norms, medicine,

19

psychology and business, man's wisdom has taken precedence over God's truth and God has been factored out. Even within the family unit there is often no acknowledgment of God. When God is factored out, the impending loss of His protection and blessing is factored in:

> Beware lest any man spoil you through philosophy and vain deceit, after the tradition of men, after the rudiments of the world, and not after Christ. For in him dwelleth all the fullness of the Godhead bodily. And ye are complete in him, which is the head of all principality and power. (Colossians 2:8-10)

People may choose to ignore God's Word in their minds, conversation and lifestyles. However, that does not alter the truth; He is the head and ultimate authority, and only by His mercy is His judgment being held back for a time. Turning away *from* God and turning *to* man for the solutions to life's dilemmas will result in bringing destruction to ourselves as the following scriptures portray:

> Thus saith the Lord; Cursed be the man that trusteth in man, and maketh flesh his arm, and whose heart departeth from the Lord. For he shall be like the heath in the desert, and shall not see when good cometh; but shall inhabit the parched places in the wilderness, in a salt land and not inhabited. Blessed is the man that trusteth in the Lord, and whose hope the Lord is. (Jeremiah 17:5-7)

The System

Resorting to man's wisdom to find a remedy for the multitudes of emotionally crippled citizens of our nation has led to the emergence of a very elaborate *system* of evaluating, diagnosing and treating individuals who suffer from what has been termed "mental disorders." This *system* is in agreement with the philosophy of secular humanism because psychology and psychiatry in general disregard the spiritual aspect of man. Psychology and psychiatry also generally exclude religion or God as a consideration in the remedy or cure for individuals with mental disorders.

Kaplan and Sadock's Synopsis of Psychiatry: Behavioral Sciences, Clinical Psychiatry (referred to from this point on as *Synopsis),* is a textbook designed for use by ". . . medical students, psychiatric residents, practicing psychiatrists, and mental health professionals" (Kaplan viii). The foundation for the current theoretical approaches and subsequent practices in the fields of psychology and psychiatry are the product of a great deal of research in the psychosocial sciences. According to Synopsis, the studies that have been done and those currently in progress are an ". . . attempt to answer questions relating to the causes, treatment, course, prognosis, and prevention of various [mental] disorders" (Kaplan 192).

Chapter four of this textbook, "Contributions of the Psychosocial Sciences to Human Behavior*,*" clarified the impediments to clinical and epidemiological studies in psychiatry: "Most studies are experimental in design; however, because of the many variables involved in mental disorders, it is difficult to design well-controlled experimental studies" (Kaplan 192). The lack of control of the variables in most studies in psychiatry leads to a questionable validity and applicability of the data and conclusions drawn from these experiments. In addition, to the best of my knowledge, not even one of the experiments cited in *Synopsis* attempts to answer what influence spirituality may have on a participant's thinking and/or behavior.

The true validity of any research depends upon the control of as many variables as possible. Both good and evil spirits, though invisible to the human eye, are determinant, if not the most significant variables influencing the thoughts and actions of all men. Since researchers in the psychosocial sciences neither understand nor have the ability to control this variable, they negate the relevance of spirituality as if it does not exist. Yet, in contemplating the basis of mental health, the "spirit world" is too consequential to be relegated to the realm of nonexistence.

Attempting studies to gain reliable and relevant knowledge about mental, emotional or behavioral disorders without any consideration of the spirit of man or the spiritual influences in our world is like attempting to determine the direction a flag blows without any consideration of the wind.

Man is more than mind and body; he does have a spirit. The world we inhabit is more than just earth and the living forms that reside here. Spiritual forces, both good and evil, dynamically and directly influence the mind of man, and this factor must be reckoned with rather than ignored. **Is it possible that a person's response to the spiritual influences in our world is the most significant factor in determining that individual's state of mental health?** Even when an emotional problem seems to be directly related to an organic cause, wisdom dictates a consideration of the spiritual influences that are operating within the scope of the problem. For example, it is not uncommon for Christians to be under greater spiritual attack when they are physically ill or exhausted. Whether a mental affliction is caused by stress, emotional pain, a physiological problem or a spiritual attack and/or oppression, a spiritual dynamic exists, which must not be disregarded.

The acknowledgment of the existence of spiritual influences in men's perceptions, thoughts and emotions opens the door for another remedy or dimension of recovery from mental afflictions. Any individual who not only acknowledges there is a God, but who also comes to the conclusion that he needs God in his life, has gained a liberating perspective of life. The knowledge of man's need for God defies the philosophy of secular humanism, which purports that man is a god unto himself, and dethrones "self." Satan quakes when an individual looks beyond "self" to God for answers to problems in life. He fears that same individual will gain the knowledge of eternal life, ultimately defeating Satan in his conquest to destroy not only that individual, but also many others who will be converted through his testimony.

A Scriptural Philosophy of Life

The Bible is a book that contains the Word of God, and though penned by men, the Bible was inspired by God. The Bible has been described as the "living Word," which no man can read and remain unchanged. The man who is humble and has a repentant heart will read and obey the Word of God, and his life will be transformed by the righteousness of Christ in him. Another man reading the same book with a proud and arrogant mind will reject the Word of God as truth and will also be changed. His character will be corrupted and his heart hardened.

When a Christian determines to live his life according to scriptural principles, he is practicing a biblical philosophy of life. Bible philosophy is simply choosing to view life through the knowledge of God as revealed to man through His Word and by His Spirit. According to Proverbs 1:7, "The fear of the Lord is the beginning of knowledge: but fools despise wisdom and instruction." Searching the Word of God and seeking God's counsel in prayer will be the avenue to obtain a scriptural perspective of life. Christians must settle in their minds that the Word of God is the ultimate authority and source of truth, and therefore, any knowledge or counsel that does not agree with that truth must be rejected.

Scriptural truths are simple enough for even a child to gain knowledge of eternal life through them (II Timothy 3:15). The only prerequisite to being able to understand the Scriptures is a humble and repentant heart. An individual's philosophy of life can be either Bible-centered or world-centered; it cannot be both, as they are opposed. A person's philosophy of life will ultimately determine what source of strength and help he will rely upon.

The Bible is the main resource used in this book for guidance to individuals with emotional problems. Ongoing comparisons of current psychiatric practices and a scriptural perspective of the same subject matter will be made throughout the book. A comparison of the two perspectives will enable the reader to form his own decisions about how to approach his circumstances in life. The reader will notice a sharp contrast between the *simplicity* of scriptural truths and the *complexity* of the terminology and information pertaining to psychiatric practices. Equally as obvious will be the *speculative* nature of the information presented in references from psychiatric works as opposed to the *authoritative* nature of the Word of God.

Bible truth will never be disproved nor made void. The principles and validity of the truth in the Word of God will not change from decade to decade or from century to century. God's Word will stand forever (Isaiah 40:8).

Chapter Three

The Simplicity of the Unchanging Christ

> But I fear, lest by any means, as the serpent beguiled Eve through his subtlety, so your minds should be corrupted from the simplicity that is in Christ. (II Corinthians 11:3)

In the last two decades scientific research has led to a proliferation of reports in psychiatric, medical and neurological journals. The data and conclusions from this research have resulted in significant changes in the field of psychiatry. According to *Synopsis,* for over a century the classic theoretical model for classifying psychiatric disorders was that they were either organic or functional in origin. *Synopsis* further indicated that current research has led to the conclusion that the organic/functional theoretical model is outdated and unsupported. Therefore, Kaplan and Sadock pointed out that in the 1994 edition of the *Diagnostic and Statistical Manual of Mental Disorders* (DSM-IV), the classic but unsupported distinction between organic and functional psychiatric disorders has been removed and replaced with diagnostic nomenclature consistent with current clinical data (336).

What the authors of *Synopsis* were saying is that from the time of Sigmund Freud in the 1880s until the 1980s, the theoretical organic/functional model for classifying psychiatric disorders was in their words, "misleading" (Kaplan 336). Perhaps it would be more correct to have said that the theoretical model was erroneous.

Speculations are Not Absolutes

Current data and reports from medical, neurological and psychiatric sources concerning the organic basis of psychiatric disorders, have led to the support of new diagnostic criteria and the reclassifying of psychiatric disorders. Kaplan and Sadock suggested that, "No unbiased evaluation of the available data could reach any other conclusion than that every psychiatric disorder has an organic (that is, biological) component" (336). Since this theory is the basis for most of the current medication interventions used in the treatment of psychiatric disorders, one would assume that the organic or biological causes for the various mental disorders has been clearly identified. This, however, is not the case. In fact, the opposite is true, as according to the authors of *Synopsis*, the cause of most mental disorders is not known (Kaplan 612).

The current theory (speculation) that every psychiatric disorder has a biological component is spoken of as if it were a statement of absolute truth when in fact the current theory may be as misleading or erroneous as was the organic/functional model that prevailed for the last century. Dr. Peter Breggin, a psychiatrist who, ". . . has held teaching appointments at Harvard Medical School, the

Washington School of Psychiatry, George Mason University, and John Hopkins University," is a well-known critic of the current theory of biological psychiatry (Breggin 217). Dr. Breggin and coauthor Dr. David Cohen made the following statements in their book, *Your Drug May Be Your Problem: How and Why to Stop Taking Psychiatric Medications*:

> . . . [N]o biochemical imbalances have ever been documented with certainty in association with any psychiatric diagnosis. The hunt goes on for these illusive imbalances; but their existence is pure speculation, inspired by those who advocate drugs.

> Even if some emotional problems turned out to be caused by subtle, as-yet-undetected biochemical imbalances, this finding would not be a rational justification for using any of the psychiatric drugs that are currently available. Because they impair normal brain function, such drugs only add to any existing brain malfunction. (34-35)

Speculation is the product of incomplete knowledge and is based on theory rather than demonstrable proof. It is important to remember that the research and conclusions of today will be outdated tomorrow, hence the need for subsequent revisions and new editions of scientific, medical and psychiatric textbooks. The incomplete knowledge base in the field of psychiatry is readily apparent in the following statement found in chapter three of *Synopsis*, "The Brain and Behavior:"

Although the brain continues to *mystify* and *inspire awe* in both lay people and neuroscientists, the innovative techniques of contemporary basic and clinical psychiatric research are rapidly *revealing* the functional organization of the human brain.
(Kaplan 87) (Italics mine)

In the preface of *Synopsis* the authors chose to quote from a presidential proclamation a description of the dilemma Americans are facing with regard to mental health issues:

Over the years, our understanding of the brain—how it works, what goes wrong when it is injured or diseased—has increased dramatically. *However, we still have much more to learn.* The need for continued study of the brain is compelling: millions of Americans are affected each year by disorders of the brain ranging from neurogenetic diseases to degenerative disorders such as Alzheimer's, as well as stroke, schizophrenia, autism, and impairments of speech, language, and hearing. (Kaplan vii) (Italics mine)

The authors of Synopsis concur with the preceding position, that the need for continued study of the brain is compelling. They predict that we are entering a new era of discovery with regard to the brain and they are in hopes that the knowledge gained will lead to "a continued improvement in the diagnosis and treatment of mental disorders" (Kaplan viii).

On the basis of the information included in this chapter, one could conclude that within the framework of science and psychiatry, there is an incomplete knowledge of the brain and its functioning, and likewise, there is an incomplete knowledge of the underlying causes of most mental disorders. In view of this knowledge deficit, it would seem wise for every Christian to personally evaluate, through prayer and his own observations and study, not only what may be the underlying causes of mental disorders, but also what is the most reliable and effective remedy for these disorders.

My own evaluation of the causes and treatment of mental disorders began in the late 1970s while I was employed as a psychiatric nursing instructor. Teaching in a psychiatric hospital setting, I became acutely aware of the inadequacy of the treatments used for treating mental disorders. Treatments, which more often than not, failed to bring about positive changes in the patients' mental or emotional status. Throughout my career, I have worked in a variety of nursing roles and have provided care to patients who were diagnosed as having a mental disorder. In spite of the changes that have taken place in the field of psychiatry over the last two decades, I continue to be concerned and alarmed about the reliability and effectiveness of various psychiatric treatment protocols, which now consist mainly of psychotropic intervention (the use of mind/mood-altering medications). Dr. Breggin in discussing the use of psychotropics, made the following statements:

> Despite a hugely successful promotional campaign by drug companies and biological psychiatry, the effectiveness of most or all

psychiatric drugs remains difficult to demonstrate. The drugs often prove no more effective than sugar pills, or placebos—and to accomplish even these limited positive results, the clinical trials and data that they generate have to be statistically manipulated. (37)

With regard to antidepressants, one of the most frequently prescribed psychotropics, I pose this question to the reader: Do you know any individuals who are being treated with antidepressants who subsequently are free of depression? I personally have never met even one individual who is depression-free or has been cured of depression as a result of taking an antidepressant. Most individuals taking antidepressants continue to *suffer* from depression. And, some of these individuals are not able to manage full or even part-time employment or to function normally in society, in spite of ongoing changes in their medication regimen.

The Real Dilemma

Most Christians realize that the real dilemma man faces is much more than just an incomplete knowledge of the brain or of mental disorders. Under the subtle influence of spiritual wickedness, our world is experiencing an ensuing moral decline and consequently an emotional decline.

Even if scientific research revealed every structural and physiological aspect of the brain, this knowledge would still be grossly inadequate because man also has a spirit and is influenced by spiritual forces. Though man's knowledge has increased at an incredible rate, it is evident the wisdom he has gained has not afforded him emotional stability. The Bible states that man is "Ever learning, and never able to come to the knowledge of the truth" (II Timothy 3:7). In order to have access to absolute truth regarding life and the mind and emotions of man, we must first have access to God. Man's knowledge or wisdom is not the avenue that provides access to God. According to I Corinthians 1:21, "For after that in the wisdom of God the world by wisdom knew not God. . . ." God has established His own plan for man to come to know Him and to have access to His knowledge. He understands every aspect of the human body including the brain, for it was God's creative ability that brought man into existence. God does not discover new insights into the functioning of the brain from year to year. His knowledge has not changed since the beginning of time. The origin of the emotional instability mankind is experiencing and that seems to elude the scientists is easily understood through the Scriptures.

The true origin of the emotional afflictions and mental instability that man has been plagued with can be found in chapters three and four of the book of Genesis where the account of the fall of man into sin is recorded. Prior to Adam and Eve breaking God's commandment, their total knowledge base was only that which God had given to them. One could say that Adam's and Eve's minds and thoughts were pure, and that their emotions were in harmony with their knowledge. "Pure" in the sense implied here means free from knowledge that would generate evil thoughts. Adam and Eve's thought patterns were acceptable to God.

After Adam and Eve disobeyed God's commandment and had eaten the fruit from the tree of the knowledge of good and evil, their knowledge base was changed. The newly acquired knowledge of evil ultimately led to evil thoughts, actions and emotional suffering. Through the knowledge of evil, the very heart of man became corrupted as described in Jeremiah 17:9-10:

> The heart is deceitful above all things, and desperately wicked: who can know it? I the Lord search the heart, I try the reins, even to give every man according to his ways, and according to the fruit of his doings.

Evil thoughts result not only in sinful behavior, but also in the emotional suffering that accompanies sin. The perfect peace of mind Adam and Eve enjoyed in the Garden of Eden was broken by the acquisition of the knowledge of evil. This knowledge of evil encompassed a variety of new perceptions and thoughts. As a consequence of their knowledge of evil, there followed an aftermath of emotions they had never before experienced. Fear took the place of peace, and sorrow replaced joy. With the passage of time, Adam and Eve would suffer feelings of grief, despair, anxiety and all the emotions that fallen humanity can experience. When they were driven from the Garden of Eden, they no doubt felt hopelessness with the realization that they could never return to that place of tranquility where they previously communed with God (Genesis 3).

God, in His mercy, made provision for man's redemption. Likewise, He provided a remedy for mental and emotional suffering. He did not leave man without a promise of hope. God had already envisioned a plan that made provision for "Himself" to be man's source of peace, comfort, joy, strength, healing, hope, deliverance and redemption.

God has given Christians the promise of not only a spiritual mind, but also of a sound mind. Ecclesiastes 1:9 reveals that there is nothing new under the sun, and within the pages of the Holy Writ there is an answer for every affliction and emotional problem that can be experienced by any individual. God delights in comforting His people and in performing the impossible. He is, ". . . our refuge and strength, a very present help in trouble" (Psalm 46:1). God has given His children assurance through His Word and by His Spirit that we can have His peace of mind and never need to fear or despair.

Chapter Four

A Sound Mind as Portrayed by the Scriptures

For God hath not given us the spirit of fear;
but of power and of love, and of a sound mind
(II Timothy 1:7).

God's gift of the Holy Ghost empowers Christians to be
able to overcome the spirit of fear, and to possess the
attributes of power, love and a sound mind. The word
"sound" when used in reference to the mind in the
preceding scripture is defined in *Strong's Concordance* as
"discipline [or] self-control." **For a Christian, a sound
mind involves having both a disciplined mind and
having control over his impulses, emotions and desires.**
"Discipline" is "training that corrects, molds, or perfects
the mental faculties or moral character." A sound mind,
from a scriptural perspective, encompasses training or
disciplining our minds with scriptural truth to mold and
perfect our spiritual character. A Christian needs to be
disciplined in what he allows to influence his thoughts, as
well as in what thoughts he allows to prevail in his mind,
". . . bringing into captivity every thought to the obedience

of Christ" (II Corinthians 10:5). The Word of God along with the Spirit of God must guide our thoughts, perceptions, desires, emotions and actions.

Self-control, which is defined as "restraint exercised over one's own impulses, emotions, or desires," is a product of yielding to the spiritual nature of God in us and restraining—ye even crucifying our carnal nature. "[T]hey that are Christ's have crucified the flesh with the affections and lusts" (Galatians 5:24). With regard to the mind and emotions, for example, a Christian need not yield to a mental state of confusion or the emotion of fear because God has assured His children that He has "not given us the spirit of fear, but of power and of love, and of a sound mind" (II Timothy 1:7). Man's emotions were meant to be subject to his higher power of reasoning. Through repentance, man's reasoning is brought into subjection to a knowledge of the truth and the will of God. Ultimately, a Christian's actions as well as his emotional state will be determined by whether he yields to his spiritual mind or his carnal mind, "For as he thinketh in his heart, so is he. . ." (Proverbs 23:7).

Most Christians would agree that the ensuing decline of morals in our society has been at least in part due to the gradual turning *from* the wisdom of God as a guide for man's thoughts and actions *to* man's own intellectual perceptions and wisdom. Paralleling this decline has been a redefining of values by Americans. Emotions, feelings and the sensual or carnal appetites have become paramount in determining how Americans view life to the degree that they often allow their emotions and desires to override the reasoning power of their minds. For example, most people realize that alcoholism will lead to a deterioration in their physical and mental well-being, yet, they continue to drink because they like how it makes them feel.

Seeking pleasure, wanting to feel good and experience happiness while avoiding any inconvenience or suffering has become the American way of life. Our culture seems to equate mental health with happiness based on self-satisfaction, self-actualization, self-fulfillment, self-indulgence—in short, "SELF" with little or no restraint. The pursuit of self-gratification and self-indulgence has contributed to an erosion of morality and a strengthening of the ideology, "If it feels good—do it." Yet, the more Americans seek to satisfy "self," the more emotionally unstable they become. "Epidemiological surveys reveal that about one third of all Americans have had or will have a mental disorder at some time in their lives" (Kaplan 192).

In contrast, the Word of God proclaims that the way to true peace and joy is to deny "self" (an act of discipline and self-restraint) and to willingly pick up a cross, the symbol of sacrifice (Luke 9:23). Christians must meet the challenge of living a life of discipline and self-restraint in order to enjoy the promise of a sound mind. Yielding to the influences of our society would result in the same disillusionment, oppression and emotional instability in the life of a Christian that is manifested in millions of Americans.

Emotions in Command

A lack of self-control over one's emotions will often lead to emotional crippling. This is evident in people who suffer from depression. Depressed individuals habitually focus on their emotions, expressing themselves with statements about their feelings, which in turn dominates their thoughts and conclusions about life. For example:

Thought pattern. . .Conclusion
- *I feel life is hopeless. . . therefore life is hopeless*
- *I feel so depressed. . . therefore I am depressed*
- *I feel like I want to die. . . therefore I want to die*

These individuals' thought patterns are predominantly based on the emotions of hopelessness and despair. They are, for the most part, unable to perceive anything good or positive in their surroundings or in life. My own experience during the years I was depressed (oppressed) was that I continually focused on my emotions throughout each day and subsequently would entertain the same question repeatedly in my mind: *How do I feel?* My perceptions about my life or circumstances were then based on the emotions I felt at any given moment.

Another example of emotions dictating conclusions is the pessimistic individual who seemingly is unable to perceive or acknowledge any positive aspect of a circumstance even if the "good" of the circumstance is much more apparent than the "bad." This individual will habitually express himself with statements such as,

- *I feel as if I will never get ahead*
- *I feel as if nobody cares about me*
- *I just feel like this will never work*

Again, this individual's thought patterns and conclusions about life are controlled by his feelings (emotions) and ultimately dictate the self-defeating behaviors that fulfill his pessimistic predictions for his life.

Perhaps, when a person feels like he is having a "nervous breakdown," this is the result of his yielding completely to his negative emotions as the dominant factor influencing his thinking. During the years I was depressed, I progressively focused more and more on my emotions to the point that the feelings of hopelessness and despair dominated my thinking during every waking moment of the day. My rational or spiritual thoughts were continually short-circuited by my emotions and the spiritual oppression I was experiencing.

In general, psychiatric counseling sessions *encourage the practice of focusing on emotions*. The overworked theory dominating most counseling sessions is that of "getting people in touch with their emotions." Envision any counseling or support group session you may have been involved in, and you will most likely remember hearing this question asked repeatedly: *"How does that make you feel?"* Emotionally crippled individuals do not need to get more in touch with their emotions—they are already enslaved by their emotions. What these individuals need to do is to get more in touch with the reasoning power of their mind and to take control of their emotions through positive, disciplined thought patterns.

Psychotropic medications hinder disciplined thought patterns because these medications alter or blunt not only a person's emotions, but likewise his ability to reason. In the book *Your Drug may Be Your Problem*, Dr. Breggin in describing the overall effect of psychiatric drugs, made the following statement:

> When a person's emotions are altered by drugs, the effect is not limited to the emotion-regulating centers of the brain. Indeed, since

the brain is a highly integrated organ, and since the drugs cause widespread disruptions within it, emotional suffering cannot be dulled without harming other functions such as concentration, alertness, sensitivity, and self-awareness. (36)

Emotional Stability Through Discipline and Self-control

The natural man experiences his world through his senses, but the interpretation of that information is determined by his knowledge, experiences, philosophy of life, emotions and established thought patterns. A Christian's frame of reference takes him into another dimension of perception that is dependent upon both his knowledge of the Scriptures and his faith. He is able to transcend in his spiritual mind what appears to be the apparent result of a negative circumstance and see a totally different outcome. No matter how negative a circumstance may be, God, responding to a Christian's faith, changes the ultimate outcome to something positive. "And we know that *all things work together for good* to them that love God, to them who are the called according to his purpose" (Romans 8:28) (Italics mine).

The Bible teaches that a mind that is disciplined with scriptural truth will produce emotional stability. According to Isaiah 26:3-4, "Thou wilt keep him in perfect peace, whose mind is stayed on thee: because he trusteth in thee. Trust ye in the Lord forever: for in the Lord JEHOVAH is everlasting strength." The word "stayed" according to *Strong's Concordance* means to "lean upon or take hold of." A disciplined mind that is stayed on God and His truth will yield perfect peace of mind. A man whose perception and thinking is guided by the Scriptures has a trust and confidence in God, being assured of God's love and care for him. He has both a knowledge of God and a knowledge of himself in relation to God.

According to Daniel 11:32, ". . . the people that do know their God shall be strong, and do exploits." Knowing God in a scriptural sense is more than just knowing He exists. There are three adjectives that can be used only in reference to God and those three adjectives and there definitions are as follows:

- Omniscient—"having infinite awareness, understanding, and insight; [or] possessed of universal or complete knowledge" [God is all knowing]
- Omnipotent—"having virtually unlimited authority or influence" [God is all powerful and has supreme authority]
- Omnipresent—"present in all places at all times" [God is present everywhere, always]

For a child of God, knowing God means realizing that all of life's experiences are channeled directly through His hands and that ultimately He is in control. Knowing God also encompasses a "God consciousness" an awareness of His constant presence through which one receives strength whether in the form of peace, comfort, boldness, courage or ability. Therefore, people who "know" their God shall be strong and do "exploits." They have disciplined their minds to perceive life and all circumstances in view of their God and His truth. They have a scripturally-based orientation to life and therefore do not easily fall prey to the deceptive devices of Satan.

Satan's Deception Leads to Oppression

The construction of Satan's web of deception is dependent upon man's carnal mind and imagination. Vulnerability to Satan's seduction is usually related to man's desires and/or fears. In the case of desires, Satan, through the power of suggestion, presents words, images and possible circumstances evoking temptation for an individual. Satan understands the process of the conception of sinful thoughts leading to sinful behavior:

> Let no man say when he is tempted, I am tempted of God: for God cannot be tempted with evil, neither tempteth he any man: But every man is tempted, when he is drawn away of his own lust, and enticed. Then when lust hath conceived, it bringeth forth sin: and sin, when it is finished, bringeth forth death. (James 1:13-15).

Sin produces guilt and emotional suffering as it always has from the beginning when Adam and Eve first sinned.

In the case of fear, Satan targets an individual's mind with suggestions, images or circumstances which evoke the emotion of fear. Fear hinders a positive approach to circumstances. Fear is the opposite of faith and leads to doubt and unbelief, resulting in a greater degree of emotional suffering. Isaiah 54:14 brings to light the link between fear and oppression: "In righteousness shalt thou be established: thou shalt be far from oppression; for thou shalt not fear: and from terror; for it shall not come near thee." The cumulative effect of sin, doubt and unbelief

44

increases an individuals vulnerability to other deceptions of Satan and, hence, to greater spiritual oppression. The act of "oppression" is defined as the "unjust or cruel exercise of authority or power" and the feeling associated with oppression as "a sense of being weighed down in body or mind: DEPRESSION." **The concept of depression, which has become so commonplace in our world today, is not merely a product of negative life experiences, but is also a result of spiritual "oppression."**

The vicious cycle of sin, oppression and emotional suffering continues until it is broken by repentance, deliverance and forgiveness by God. The spiritual battle we are engaged in is ". . . not against flesh and blood, but against principalities, against powers, against the rulers of the darkness of this world, against spiritual wickedness in high places" (Ephesians 6:12). At this point, I want to reiterate a question that was posed in chapter two: **Is it possible that a person's response to the spiritual influences in our world is the most significant factor in determining that individual's state of mental health (22)?** I believe an individual's response to the Spirit of God or to Satan's demonic influence will determine his peaceful or tormented state of mind. God has promised to keep us in perfect peace if our minds are stayed upon Him. Conversely, any individual whose mind is oppressed by the "rulers of the darkness of this world" will be tormented.

Light or Darkness

Darkness in a natural sense shrinks a person's world much the same as a prison cell. Options are restricted and possibilities are not apparent, as the physical senses are limited. The reaction of straining to compensate for the reduction in perception through the senses results in a heightened imagination. A state of heightened imagination usually produces fear and confusion. Darkness, fear and confusion are characteristic of Satan's domain.

The opposite of a God-given peace of mind is a mind that is ravaged by fear, torment and despair. While working in home care as a nurse, I took care of a woman who suffered from both physical and mental problems. Engraved on my mind is the memory of the spiritual darkness that encompassed this woman. Upon entering the woman's apartment for my initial visit, I made a request for a light to be turned on, though it was the middle of the day. The woman turned on a light in the adjacent room where she was sitting; yet, the apartment still seemed dark. Glancing around the kitchen where I was standing before proceeding to the next room, I sensed an overwhelming aura of gloom and despair saturating the apartment.

While my eyes were adjusting to the darkness, I peered through the kitchen to the dining room where there were black curtains closed over the windows obstructing any natural daylight from entering the room. Turning to the right as I walked in the direction of the woman's voice, I entered the living room and observed there were black drapes closed over the windows in that room. The woman's countenance matched her surroundings. She had fashioned her apartment to reflect the state of her mind and in so doing, increased the darkness in her mind. This woman was in a battle with the "rulers of darkness of this world" and was losing the battle. Humanity alone is no match for "spiritual wickedness in high places" (Ephesians 6:12). The object of Satan's onslaught within the battlefield of the mind is to bring darkness and the accompanying fear, confusion and deception. A mind can be filled with darkness, or a mind can be filled with light as portrayed in Matthew 6:22-23:

> The light of the body is the eye: if therefore thine eye be single, thy whole body shall be full of light. But if thine eye be evil, thy whole body shall be full of darkness. If therefore the light that is in thee be darkness, how great is that darkness!

The Bible teaches us that Jesus is the Light that shines in darkness and that, "In him was life; and the life was the light of men" (John 1:4-5). As mentioned previously, repentance involves changing the way one thinks. A man who has dedicated his life to Christ will discipline his mind with scriptural truths and will possess an exclusive perspective of life—his "eye is single." He will reject both the vain philosophies of men (and their imaginations) and the deceptive ideas that Satan would attempt to impose upon his mind. He will bring his thoughts into obedience to Christ by disciplining his mind with the Scriptures and by communing with Christ in a daily discipline of prayer (II Corinthians 10:5). A Christian must have a singular or undivided mind to yield perfect peace and stability of mind.

A Christian whose mind is divided and entertains two opposing philosophies—the vain philosophies of man and a scriptural philosophy—will be confused and unstable. James 1:8 describes this man as, "A double minded man is unstable in all his ways." A "double minded man" is vulnerable to deception and to the snare of the devil. Individuals who oppose themselves actually become self-destructive in both their thinking and actions. Deliverance will only come through acknowledging "truth" in the Word of God and through repentance by which they can recover themselves out of the snare of the devil (II Timothy 2:25-26). Every deceptive "stronghold" will be exposed and brought down as a Christian disciplines his mind in obedience to Christ and to the truth in the Word of God (II Corinthians 10:3-6).

Repent: To Think Differently

Repentance is based upon a change in a person's thinking (*Strong's Concordance*). A man who has a scriptural philosophy of life realizes the importance of repentance on an ongoing basis. Likewise, he realizes his need for a consistent prayer life in order to commune with God every day. Whatever experiences or difficulties he encounters during that day will be met by him acknowledging God for guidance in his decisions or actions. He has no need to fear or become anxious about the problems or difficulties that he may face.

The emotions of fear and anxiety are a product of anticipated harm or danger, whether real or fantasized. God has told His children in Philippians 4:6-8 to,

> Be careful [*anxious: Strong's Concordance*] for nothing; but in every thing by prayer and supplication with thanksgiving let your requests be made known unto God. And the peace of God, which passeth all understanding, shall keep [*guard or protect: Strong's Concordance*] your hearts and minds through Christ Jesus. Finally, brethren, whatsoever things are true, whatsoever things are honest, whatsoever things are just,

whatsoever things are pure, whatsoever things are lovely, whatsoever things are of good report; if there be any virtue, and if there be any praise, think on these things.

The preceding scriptures indicate that a Christian has the ability to possess both peace of mind and emotional stability. By bringing our problems to Jesus in prayer with a spirit of thanksgiving, He will meet our needs and give us His peace, which will protect our hearts and minds. In addition, a Christian must discipline his mind to entertain only thoughts that are true, honest, just, pure, lovely and of good report.

The "Word" Living "In" You

Many people who are trying to live a Christian life through *knowledge* of the Scriptures *alone* find themselves falling short of the spiritual victory they desire. There is a higher dimension or higher power beyond self-discipline that can yield prevailing victory. A person may have knowledge of the Scriptures by having studied the Bible and yet not be spiritually minded because he does not have the Spirit of Christ *in* him. Paul writes in Romans 8:9, "But ye are not in the flesh, but in the Spirit, if so be that the Spirit of God dwell in you. Now if any man have not the Spirit of Christ, he is none of his." An individual needs to have the Spirit of Christ dwelling in him to empower him to be able to think spiritually.

To have knowledge of the Word of God is very beneficial, but to have the *Word* living *in* you enables a Christian to live triumphantly! The Bible speaks of this

49

experience as the gift of the Holy Ghost. Having the Holy Ghost will allow an individual to experience the following:

- Have the laws of God written in his heart and mind (Hebrews 8:10; 10:16)
- Have the mind of Christ (I Corinthians 2:14-16)
- Be transformed by the renewing of his mind (Romans 12:1-2)
- Be spiritually minded, yielding life and peace (Romans 8:6)
- Serve the Lord with his mind (Romans 7:24-25)
- "Know" Him (Philippians 3:8-15)

The Holy Spirit abiding within will bring about a God consciousness and revelation of truth that far surpasses the efforts of a natural man to discipline his mind with scriptural truths. To be spiritually minded means to be able to think like Jesus because His Spirit is in us. Receiving the Holy Spirit is a promise as Acts 2:38-39 state,

> Then Peter said unto them, Repent, and be baptized every one of you in the name of Jesus Christ for the remission of sins, and ye shall receive the gift of the Holy Ghost. For the promise is unto you, and to your children, and to all that are afar off, even as many as the Lord our God shall call.

When we receive the Spirit of Christ and have taken upon ourselves His name (Jesus) in baptism, we become part of His body—the church.

And he is the head of the body, the church: who is the beginning, the firstborn from the dead; that in all things he might have the preeminence.

Who now rejoice in my sufferings for you, and fill up that which is behind of the afflictions of Christ in my flesh for his body's sake, which is the church: (Colossians 1:18; 24)

As part of the body of Christ we must continue to acknowledge the head of the body, which is Christ and to think like Him. Romans 8:6 states, "For to be carnally minded is death; but to be spiritually minded is life and peace." Being spiritually minded is dependent upon receiving Christ's Spirit, disciplining our minds with the Scriptures, daily seeking His counsel in prayer and exercising self-control in our thoughts and emotions. The Bible clearly identifies Jesus as our counselor, deliverer, advocate, healer and the one who should be guiding our thoughts—but this is still our choice to make.

Chapter Five

Strongholds Within and Without

> For though we walk in the flesh, we do not war after the flesh: (For the weapons of our warfare are not carnal, but mighty through God to the pulling down of **strong holds**;) Casting down imaginations, and every high thing that exalteth itself against the knowledge of God, and bringing into captivity every thought to the obedience of Christ. (II Corinthians 10:3-5)

II Corinthians 10:3-5 portrays the spiritual battleground in which Christians find themselves and identifies the spiritual weapon that is available to ensure their victory. The spiritual battleground for Christians is clearly in their minds, and it is only through bringing their thoughts into obedience to Christ that they will achieve and maintain victory. Likewise, the spiritual battle for those who are not Christians is also in their minds. Through repentance, bringing their thoughts into obedience to Christ, they can be liberated from the bondage of sin and the oppression of Satan.

In Luke 4:17-21 we find Jesus in the synagogue reading

from the book of Isaiah, and, after closing the book, He said to all that were present, "This day is this scripture fulfilled in your ears." Teaching in the temple that day, Jesus revealed His deity, the gift of salvation and His ministry of comfort, healing and deliverance to lost humanity. Those hearing His words comprehended only to a limited degree what He was teaching about, as Christ's earthly ministry was just beginning. He taught that through the Spirit of the Lord would come several ministries: the gospel preached to the poor, healing to the brokenhearted, deliverance to the captives, sight to the blind and liberty to the bruised. Jesus would usher in the acceptable year of the Lord as manifested through His ministry of reconciliation.

Man not only needed a Savior to provide an atoning sacrifice for his sins, but he also needed deliverance, healing and comfort. Each specific promise referred to by Jesus in Luke 4:18-19 identified a source of God's provision designed to meet the needs of humanity.

The gospel—the "good news" concerning the atoning sacrifice and plan of salvation that was shortly to be accomplished through Christ's crucifixion—would be preached to the spiritually destitute. Through the gospel would come deliverance to those held in captivity, bound by the chains of sin. The promise of recovered sight to the blind could, of course, be referring to physical blindness as Jesus did restore sight to the blind who sought healing from Him; however, I believe this reference is also applicable to spiritual blindness. Jesus is the true Light that shines in darkness, and those who receive His Spirit will become the children of light, dispelling the darkness that is associated with spiritual blindness (John 1:5; 12:35).

Deliverance from captivity, healing for the brokenhearted and liberty for the bruised encompasses the provisions necessary to restore to wholeness those who have suffered emotional trauma and who are emotionally unstable. The definition of the word "bruise" when referring to the mind means to "wound," "injure" [or] "to inflict psychological hurt on." Individuals who have been wounded emotionally need emotional healing and liberation from spiritual oppression.

Oppression, as mentioned in chapter four of this book, has a dual meaning: The mental or emotional aspect of oppression, "a sense of being weighed down in body or mind; DEPRESSION" and the act of oppression, "unjust or cruel exercise of authority or power." An emotionally crippled individual is held in captivity by "**strong holds**" from both within and without. Inwardly, his habitually negative thought patterns of hopelessness hold him captive, and outwardly, the oppressive influence of satanic forces against his mind enforce his captivity. These two aspects of oppression stand as the seemingly impenetrable inner and outer walls of a fortress. According to *Strong's Concordance*, the words "strong holds" (found in II Corinthians 10:4) mean a fortification or a fortress, usually symbolic of the walls surrounding a city or castle that are meant to secure and protect those within the walls (spelled stronghold in *Webster's Dictionary*). However, when referring to the thoughts and mind of man as was portrayed in that verse of scripture the words "strong holds" represent walls of spiritual oppression that surround an individual. These walls do not represent protection, but rather typify a prison or place of captivity fortified by oppressive forces within and without as explained above. Consider these scriptures again,

For though we walk in the flesh, we do not war after the flesh: (For the weapons of our warfare are not carnal, but mighty through God to the pulling down of strong holds;) Casting down imaginations, and every high thing that exalteth itself against the knowledge of God, and bringing into captivity every thought to the obedience of Christ. (II Corinthians 10:3-5)

The "strong holds" are associated with imaginations and thoughts that are against, or in opposition to, the knowledge of God. God alone knows all things, including the beginning and the ending of all circumstances. Thought patterns that are born out of a person's carnal perceptions, imaginations, conclusions, reasoning and understanding form the strong holds that exist within a man's mind. Victory over the strong holds is dependent upon thinking the thoughts Christ would have him think, thoughts that would be in agreement with the Word of God.

In addition, there are also the deceptive ideas that Satan attempts to impose on an individual's mind. Through subtlety, Satan attempts to persuade man to accept his deceptive ideas concerning himself, others, God, life or circumstances. Over time, the acceptance of these ideas solidifies into habitual thought patterns, causing an individual to progressively become more vulnerable to the control of the "deceiver," thus paving the way for greater deception and oppression. Satan's objective is to monopolize a person's thinking and emotions and, therefore, his actions. His ultimate goal would be to totally control or possess an individual and thereby orchestrate his doom. Satan's influence upon man's mind is always against the knowledge of God, and the degree to which a person accepts Satan's ideas as truth secures Satan's oppression over him.

Whatever the origin, these spiritual "strong holds" must be pulled down. Jesus knows what strong holds exist in a person's mind, how they were constructed and the misconceptions, deceptions and negative thought patterns that continue to reinforce the walls of deception holding him captive. He understands the demonic forces that operate to fortify Satan's oppression. If there is a physiological component contributing to one's emotional instability that would prevent the peace and joy of a sound mind, God is likewise completely aware of that element and has promised to heal all of our diseases (Psalm 103:3). Through deliverance and healing Jesus will set the captive free.

Even Christians may become oppressed if they do not guard their minds and keep their thoughts stayed on Jesus and His truth. Children of God have received Christ's Spirit and subsequently possess both a spiritual and a carnal mind. The attack of the adversary, Satan, is directed toward a Christian's carnal mind with the intent to bring him back into the captivity from which he has been set free. The following testimony of my descent into oppression and my deliverance from a prison of hopelessness will portray both spiritual forces of "good" and "evil" that operate in this world.

Descent Into Oppression

I choose not to describe the circumstances that led to my emotional instability and crippling. There are many things in life that can precipitate emotional instability, including but not limited to illness, the loss of a loved one, emotional or physical abuse, failed relationships and even financial and employment circumstances. The spiritual battle I was engaged in was not against flesh and blood, but as Paul so accurately describes our battles to be, ". . . against principalities, against powers, against the rulers of the darkness of this world, against spiritual wickedness in high places" (Ephesians 6:12). The spiritual attack I endured did not take its toll quickly; only after many years did I begin to accept some of the deceiver's ideas concerning my life and future.

The gradual acceptance of these lies allowed them to become the central focus of my thoughts. These thoughts were accompanied by the emotions of hopelessness and despair. Hopelessness gradually dominated all my perceptions about life. I was unable to experience the joy that should come from relationships with my family, children and friends or my walk with God, my work in the church and even from the beauty of nature that surrounded me. Though I had no desire to leave the church, I did not experience the satisfaction and joy that accompanies living for God.

The spiritual oppression lasted approximately six years. At the onset, the attack was very subtle, making it difficult to discern the spirit that was oppressing me. The oppression began like the slow progression of a degenerative neurological disease. Initially, I was able to compensate for the changes in my thinking and my emotions, and though I was gradually becoming more oppressed, I was almost unaware of the changes in my personality and moods. However, as time wore on, the emotional crippling advanced to such a degree that every area of my life was deteriorating, including my health, job, relationships with friends and loved ones and my walk with God. Finally, even the desire to live left me.

I could not understand why the Lord was allowing the years of suffering that I endured. I prayed fervently and earnestly for God to intervene, all the while believing another of Satan's deceptions—that I was to blame for the circumstances in my life.

As time passed, God slowly and gently made me aware that what I was hoping and believing for was not going to happen. God began to prepare me for events that would soon come to pass in our family. Often, when God is going to give me knowledge of something that will be difficult for me to receive, He will wake me up in the middle of the night and impress a thought on my mind. The following account describes one such occasion when the Lord spoke to me to prepare me for the fiery trial that I would be going through in the near future.

One night I was awakened, and the Lord impressed this message on my mind: *Your marriage is never going to be what you want it to be . . .* Simultaneously came the reality of the finality of the message. I knew the Lord had spoken to me. Fear and despair gripped my heart. I got out of bed, went to the living room, dropped to my knees and began to weep. I wept and poured out my heart to God, trying to accept what seemed like total devastation for our family. I was unaware of time, and hours passed as I continued to pray in an effort to lay my broken heart on the altar.

Then, as if someone slipped a warm blanket around me, a feeling of peace enveloped my soul. I rose from that place of prayer and went back to the bedroom and lay down. Moments later the second half of the Lord's message came as clearly as if He had spoken the words out loud . . . *but, I will make the difference.* I wish I could say that the feeling of peace continued and that I rode above the rest of the storm and trial with an ever-present victory, but I cannot. In fact, after this experience, I began to sink deeper and deeper into despair. I had lost the hope for the miracle that I had "designed" and that I had been clinging to for so many years. Sometimes our self-conceived miracles, the product of our hopes and desires, are more focused on ourselves than on God.

I did not realize the degree of spiritual oppression that I had become vulnerable to, nor did I recognize that the thought patterns of hopelessness were a spiritual stronghold in my mind. Though I continued to pray, take care of my family, be faithful to church and work my job, it seemed as if there were a cloud hovering over me. As months passed the cloud became larger and darker until I was completely engulfed by the darkness.

I knew that as a Christian I would face many spiritual battles. I had personally experienced many victories as a child of God and yet, I could not seem to rise above this cloud. The intensity of the oppression increased to such a degree that during every waking moment and even in dreams at night the devil was able to oppress and torment my mind.

In order for Satan to be able to gain this type of control there must be an inroad into a Christian's mind and, subsequently, his heart. The Bible states,

> In righteousness shalt thou be established: thou shalt be far from oppression; for thou shalt not fear: and from terror; for it shall not come near thee. (Isaiah 54:14)

There is no fear in love; but perfect love
casteth out fear: because fear hath torment.
He that feareth is not made perfect in love.
(I John 4:18)

Whether Satan's control is gained through fear, confusion,
doubt, unbelief, disobedience, unthankfulness, hatred, lust,
pride or money, there is a stronghold of deception in a
person's mind that has allowed Satan to oppress him.

My vulnerability to the oppression of Satan was related
to unforgiveness, though it would have been virtually
impossible for another person to have convinced me of this
fact, for I truly believed I had been forgiving. The Lord
chose to reveal my unforgiving spirit through a sermon that
dealt with the subject of forgiving. The minister explained
that it is much more difficult to forgive than to ask for
forgiveness and that an individual who will not forgive is in
great danger of losing his soul. Through this sermon, God
was preparing my mind to receive a revelation that would
ultimately lead to my deliverance.

Breaking the Yoke of Spiritual Oppression

During the altar call following the sermon, I prayed to
God for an answer to why I was so depressed. I do not
know why I had not asked the Lord about the cause of my
depression before this time. My perspective was probably
more aligned with the concepts I had learned in psychology
courses in college; therefore, I did not consider my
depression to be of a spiritual nature.

After asking the Lord what was causing my depression,
the impression came to me that I was unforgiving. As I
continued to pray I disputed this with the Lord. The

impression was still the same—God was revealing my unforgiving heart. Realizing that God knows all things, I accepted His admonition and offered this plea: *"If this is true Lord, then apparently I am not able to forgive any more. Lord, please do a divine work of forgiveness in me."* On the basis of my willingness to ask for and receive that miracle, God performed a miracle in my heart.

I would also like the reader to know that the forgiveness I needed to extend at this time was more toward God than toward any person. It was apparent that I needed to forgive people, but it was not apparent that I had judged God for the circumstances that existed in my life. Something inside of me had yielded to the deception that God not only could have, but should have, changed those circumstances. I did not realize until approximately two years later what had really transpired in my heart that night as God performed the miracle I had requested.

This was only the beginning of my deliverance. With that miracle performed, God then chose to reveal to me what had been tormenting me day and night for years. His method of revealing the oppression of Satan was very unusual. I had what might be considered a vision within a dream.

Early one morning I awoke and, though alert, it seemed I was still asleep and dreaming. I leaned over the side of the bed and saw one of my *Country Living* magazines on the floor. Next to the magazine was a small rectangular wall mirror with the cardboard back facing up. I pressed my hand against the mirror, and it held fast. Lifting the mirror, I turned it over to view my face. In the depth of the mirror behind where the reflection of my face should have been, but was not, was a horrifying image. I cannot recall any of the details of the image except my perception of the extreme evil personified in the face. Speaking in a calm voice, I asked, *"Lord, what is that?"* Quickly an answer came to me: *It is a demon of depression.* I felt no fear while viewing the image, nor did I feel any fear once I understood the image was the face of a demon. Rather, there was a sense of relief to finally know what I had been battling for years. At this point in time, I realized I was fully awake, and the memory of the experience was more like a vision than a dream. God had revealed to me not only that I was oppressed, but also the source of the oppression.

What I thought was "depression" was in fact a "demonic oppression." Recognizing the problem as spiritual oppression made the remedy to the problem very clear—I needed deliverance. Though it seemed impossible as a child of God to be suffering from this type of oppression, nevertheless, I was. I determined to seek God for deliverance at the next church service, yet in retrospect I realize I could have been delivered that very morning by just praying to God for deliverance.

The next Sunday morning church service was an unforgettable experience. Shortly after the singing started, a spirit of worship moved over the congregation. Intercessory prayer then followed. As the prayer subsided, a quietness prevailed that was broken by a message in tongues and an interpretation. The Lord declared Himself to be our deliverer and further told the church that if we would come to Him, He would deliver us. Immediately I left the place where I was sitting and made my way to the front of the church to pray.

After perhaps 45 minutes of fervent prayer, I became confused because I did not feel anything that would indicate I had been delivered. Discouraged, I left the altar area and walked slowly out the back doors of the sanctuary into the vestibule where one of my closest friends was standing. I questioned her about why I did not feel anything after praying so hard and so long. She said, *"You don't have to feel anything to be delivered."* I knew this to be true; but it was very important for me to know I was delivered.

Reentering the sanctuary where the altar service continued, I prayed that the miracle of deliverance would be confirmed as I said, *"Lord, I don't have to feel anything to be delivered, but I need to know I am delivered. If I am delivered, please let the organist play the song, Sing Unto the Lord a New Song."* The organist was playing a song, which he ended rather abruptly. He began to play some chords as if not sure what song to play. The next chords he played were from the song, *Sing Unto the Lord a New Song!*

With my deliverance confirmed, I joyously worshiped the Lord. That night I walked out of the church delivered from the oppression of Satan and the prison of hopelessness that had held me captive for six long years. The experience was like coming back to life from the grave. The Lord continued to perfect my understanding about the great work of deliverance He had performed in my life.

One week after the service in which I received my deliverance, our church began having revival services. On the second night of the revival when the guest minister took the service, he explained that he felt led of the Spirit to do some teaching on spiritual oppression. He began by describing some of the circumstances that he had encountered in his own congregation. Apparently, he had noticed that there were several faithful and established members in his church who did not appear to have any joy in their walk with God. He could see despair, sadness and even depression on their countenances. One of the individuals also suffered from constant pain for which her physician could identify no organic cause. Being led of the Lord, he began to pray, fast and seek God for those individuals. In response to his petitions, the Lord revealed to him that each of them was experiencing spiritual oppression. At this point in his teaching, he explained that he did not like to use the words "demonic oppression" because it made people feel uncomfortable to think they were demonically oppressed. Therefore, he chose to use the term "spiritually oppressed," as this was more readily received. He went on to explain that arrangements were made with each of these individuals separately to discuss what the Lord had revealed to him about spiritual oppression and to request that he and his wife be allowed to pray with them and for them.

The woman who was experiencing both emotional suffering and physical pain received her pastor's explanation and expressed her relief to understand that she had been battling spiritual oppression. When her pastor and his wife prayed with her, she was completely delivered; she was free to experience the joy of her salvation and she no longer suffered from pain. The pastor stated that while praying for her, he saw something that appeared like a faint black shadow lift up off her. Although she suffered from both mental and physical oppression, what she needed was deliverance—not healing—since the cause of the pain was not related to a physical problem, but rather was due to spiritual oppression.

Subsequent to the pastor's meetings with the other church members concerning their experience of spiritual oppression, each individual was delivered. His teaching brought relief and clarity concerning my own experience of oppression and deliverance. I had felt ashamed to think that I had been demonically oppressed. God had sent this minister to prevent any further deception that Satan would attempt to impose upon my mind as a result of thinking negatively about myself as a Christian. I needed this instruction since I had never heard of any other church members who were spiritually oppressed. Through this experience came both an understanding of what spiritual oppression is and the knowledge that God's deliverance and healing is the remedy for spiritual oppression as well as emotional crippling. This experience became a pillar of strength to me in my walk with God.

In summary, all people including Christians need to recognize that the indoctrination of our society with psychiatric terminology, principles and treatments, has afforded Satan an opportunity to disguise his oppressive control over people's minds. Satanic oppression, once exposed for what it is through the truth in the Word of God, will be defeated by the power of Christ to set people free!

Chapter Six

Dialogue: The Unguarded Front

On a daily basis Christians may be exposed to influences which could hinder spiritually disciplined thought patterns. Indiscretion by Christians regarding the influences they subject their minds to will ultimately affect their thoughts, beliefs and actions. One of the most significant factors influencing an individual's thought patterns is what is communicated to him through visual images as well as the spoken or written word. Amidst the information overload bombarding all people in America, it is at times very difficult to both assimilate and evaluate whether the information being presented would compromise a Christian's spiritual integrity. Nevertheless, as Christians we need to spiritually discern two things before deciding to accept or reject information being presented to us. First, the source: who or what is behind the message, and secondly, the agenda: the anticipated effect the message is meant to have on the recipient of the information. Often, both source and agenda are disguised or hidden. A Christian's sensitivity to the Spirit of God and his knowledge of the Scriptures will be his weapons of warfare in this battle.

God has given Christians His Spirit to act as a filter in their minds to enable them to separate out the impurities of the influences that would pollute their thoughts. If every influence is construed to be a voice that could speak to our minds, then Jesus will be the "Caller ID" of our minds, given that we are sensitive to Him and have disciplined our minds to bring every thought into obedience to Him. His still small voice will tell us that the caller or message should be rejected, deleted or erased. Sensitivity to the Spirit of God is dependent upon our daily communion with Him through prayer and through reading the Word of God. Prayerlessness and neglect in reading and studying the Bible will result in carnal thinking and ultimately an insensitivity to His voice.

> For to be carnally minded is death; but to be spiritually minded is life and peace. Because the carnal mind is enmity against God: for it is not subject to the law of God, neither indeed can be. (Romans 8:6-7)

> For as many as are led by the Spirit of God, they are the sons of God. (Romans 8:14)

During a time when I was going through one of the deepest spiritual/emotional trials of my life, many voices came to me encouraging me to take antidepressant medication, but the still small voice within me (my spiritual caller ID), made it clear that I was to reject that remedy and turn to Jesus for His help in my time of trouble.

As was previously mentioned, Christians need to consider both the source of the information being presented and the agenda or anticipated effect the information is intended to have upon them. Once these two things are exposed or discerned, a Christian is able to make an informed choice as to whether or not the information is to be accepted or rejected. There are two circumstances in which Christians or, for that matter, all people are more vulnerable to being deceived or negatively influenced by the source or the agenda behind information being presented to them.

First, is the circumstance when information is presented through "authorities" such as: educators, physicians, scientists, lawyers, counselors, government officials or politicians who we consider to be more knowledgeable than ourselves with regard to certain subjects. The second circumstance in which a Christian may be more vulnerable to deception is when engaged in a conversation format called "dialogue." Both of these circumstances pose a considerable threat to a Christian as in each of these communication formats our guard over our minds may be compromised.

Academic Sources of Information

Information from authoritative sources is disseminated in a variety of formats such as: all forms of media, conferences, lectures, books, advertisements or one-on-one conversations. Professionals who hold academic degrees or have expertise in areas in which we do not have a comparable level of education or knowledge will present their information in an authoritative manner. Often, their expectation is that the information will be received with little or no questions asked. This is true particularly in the area of psychiatry where the expectation is that both the diagnosis and the treatment protocols being presented will not be questioned by the patient.

Pharmaceutical "promos" as well as other academic sources have propagated the belief in people's minds that emotional problems are caused from chemical imbalances in the brain and that these imbalances can be corrected by use of psychotropic medications. According to Dr. Breggin, Americans believe that they are informed about the scientific research that has demonstrated a biological or genetic cause for emotional disorders, when in fact biological psychiatry is purely speculation (4-7). He further stated,

> It appears that we have replaced reliance on God, other people, and ourselves with reliance on medical doctors and psychiatric drugs. The ultimate *source* of guidance and inspiration is no longer life itself with its infinite resources but biopsychiatry with its narrow view of human nature.

> This view of ourselves is a most astonishing one. It suggests that most if not all of our psychological, emotional, and spiritual problems are "psychiatric disorders" best treated by specialists who prescribe psychoactive drugs. Our emotional and spiritual problems are not only seen as psychiatric disorders, they are declared to be biological and genetic in origin.

> The propaganda for this remarkable perspective is financed by drug companies

70

and spread by the media, by organized psychiatry and individual doctors, by "consumer" lobbies, and even by government agencies such as the National Institute of Mental Health. (4-7) (Italics mine)

In evaluating the preceding information, who is really the source behind the propaganda? Is the source behind the propaganda the drug companies or psychiatrists with an agenda of profiting tremendous financial gains? Is the source Satan, who is spreading his deceptive doctrine that the solution for man's emotional and perhaps even spiritual problems lies in man's wisdom and man's remedies? Is Satan's agenda to destroy man's confidence in God and bring eternal damnation to mankind by whatever means possible? By believing the information being disseminated by media, pharmaceutical companies, psychiatrists, and many other academic sources are we as Christians "giving heed to seducing spirits, and doctrines of devils?" (I Timothy 4:1).

Our society has been dramatically impacted by the use of psychotropics and the *theory* of biological psychiatry as well as the use of psychiatric labels to describe our emotional responses to life. Frequently, the first response to someone saying he has an emotional problem is another individual suggesting not only what he thinks the mental disorder is, but also what type of medication a physician would prescribe for treatment.

I was having lunch with several ladies from our church and one of them made the comment that her nerves were on edge. The immediate response from one of the other ladies was that she should see her doctor about getting some medicine. This advice was seconded by another woman at the table! Christians must evaluate the sources propagating this information and the underlying agenda behind it. Most Christians would probably recognize and acknowledge that mind/mood-altering drugs such as alcohol or street drugs lead to both addiction and degradation; yet, we have been persuaded to believe that prescription psychiatric medications are not only beneficial, but safe. According to Dr. Breggin:

> Psychiatric medications are, first and foremost, psychoactive or psychotropic drugs: They influence the way a person feels, thinks, and acts. Like cocaine and heroin, they change the emotional response capacity of the brain. If used to solve emotional problems, they end up shoving those problems under the rug of drug intoxication while creating additional drug-induced problems. (12)

The influence of "psychiatric terminology" has been so pervasive in our society that Americans in general view most, if not all, emotional problems as psychiatric disorders. Christians have likewise become accustomed to describing their emotions by using psychiatric jargon. Sadness or discouragement is referred to as "depression." And rather than express that we feel compelled to do certain things, we associate these feelings with compulsive behaviors. When we experience feelings that people do not like us, we describe these emotions as paranoia. The danger in using psychiatric terms to describe normal emotions is that we are more likely to view them as abnormal and to seek a remedy within the psychiatric realm.

Normal emotions that would provoke an individual to evaluate his thoughts or actions and determine the need for changes in his life are now relegated to psychiatric problems for which he needs to see a physician and obtain a medication. Even the uncomfortable feeling of conviction is spoken of by some Christians as if it were something that could be remedied by a psychotropic drug.

Dialogue: A Conduit of Deception

Dialogue is another format of communication that compromises a Christian's guard over his mind. Dialogue, discussion and debate are three methods of communication by which individuals can exchange ideas, opinions or information. The simplest definition of the word "dialogue" is "to converse." A discussion is a "consideration of a question in open and usually informal debate." Debate means, "a contention by words or arguments." Using the word "dialogue" in referring to communication carries a distinct connotation that is different from the words, "discussion" or "debate." Dialogue seems to have become the word of choice for communication whether in the arena of education, religion, politics, government or even in global affairs. What is the significance of the choice of this word when referring to communication?

Dialogue, as opposed to a discussion or a debate, affords an indulgent or tolerant format for communication between individuals who may possess opposing ideas, opinions, values or beliefs. The implication of engaging in dialogue is that there is a desire for the establishment of a common ground between the conversing parties. **Referring to the conversation as dialogue tends to disarm the participants' belief systems and values during the**

communication process. The individuals are *simply* exchanging ideas and there is not, at least on the surface, an expected outcome or agenda. Dialogue as a platform for communication masquerades as a harmless, neutral ground that is noncommittal in nature; thus, the participants' guard over their minds is compromised.

Dialogue as a "tolerant" format for communication has increased in popularity over the last two decades. Consider the following statement made by Mikhail Gorbachev in a March 9, 1992 article in the *New York Times* entitled "My Partner the Pope:"

> I have carried on an intensive correspondence with Pope John Paul II since we met at the Vatican in December 1989. I think ours will be an ongoing dialogue. The sense of mutual affection and understanding that resulted from our meeting is to be found in each of our letters. I cannot help but say that we share a desire to move forward and complete what we began together. Personally, I would be glad to take any opportunity to continue working with the Pope and I am certain that this desire is mutual and will prove lasting. (A17)

It is noteworthy that when Mr. Gorbachev referred to how he and Pope John Paul II were communicating he used the word dialogue. He alluded to the idea that they had established a common ground subsequent to their meeting and their dialogue, and that they "share" a desire to move forward and complete what they have begun.

Another notable example of a very short, yet consequential dialogue, is found in the Bible in Genesis

3:1-6. In fact, this dialogue consisted of only a few sentences. The serpent (Satan) was engaging in a dialogue with Eve. The serpent and Eve had very little in common, and their belief systems and values were diametrically opposed. Nevertheless, they pushed aside these differences to engage in what appeared to be at the onset just harmless dialogue. Eve relinquished the guard to her mind while the dialogue with her disguised adversary progressed. Satan hates God and wanted to destroy man's relationship with God, though his agenda was concealed during the course of their conversation. The serpent's subtle weapon of destruction was a brief session of dialogue. Unfortunately, Eve fell prey to the serpent's scheme (agenda) to manipulate her thinking and therefore her actions

Dr. Deborah Flick, trainer/consultant specializing in workplace diversity issues, has for over 20 years provided consultation and training "to corporations, local and federal governments, non-profits, colleges and universities, and unions" (147). In her book, *From Debate to Dialogue: Using the Understanding Process to Transform Our Conversations,* Dr. Flick discussed the criteria of an underlying attitude of openness and genuine curiosity as the basis for the "Understanding process," which is the foundation for the communication format of dialogue (21). Using Dr. Flick's criteria we are able to identify the format of communication that the serpent and Eve were engaged in, as being a format of "dialogue." Eve's mind was open and she was genuinely curious about the serpent's information regarding the tree in the midst of the garden. What harm could there be in exchanging ideas or even opinions about what God had said or meant regarding the trees in the garden and the fruit of those trees? A common ground for "sharing" was established between the serpent and Eve.

The serpent began the conversation by asking if God had said that Eve should not eat of every tree of the garden. As the conversation progressed, Satan introduced the deceptive idea that if Eve ate of the fruit of the tree in the midst of the garden, not only would she not die, but she would become as a god knowing good and evil. Eve reasoned that the tree looked desirable and decided that the fruit from that tree would be a good source of food. Eve had been seduced during the course of the conversation (dialogue) to believe that the fruit from the tree in the midst of the garden had some kind of power to make her "wise" (Genesis 3:1-6). The end result of this short session of dialogue was far different from what Eve had anticipated.

There are times when dialogue would be the format of choice for some conversations; but depending upon the subject matter and the communicating participants, discussion, debate or no communication at all would be a more appropriate course of action. In chapter two of *From Debate to Dialogue,* Dr. Flick explained that the understanding process "assumes that there are *multiple, valid perspectives on any given matter, yours included.* No one person or point of view contains the whole 'truth' about the matter at hand" (19). However, concerning the subject matter that Eve and the serpent were discussing, God alone knew the ***whole truth*** about the consequences of eating the fruit from the tree in the midst of the garden. For Christians there is an ultimate and final authority whose *Word* is truth. There are not multiple, valid perspectives on any given matter, but rather there are absolutes in the Word of God that are to govern a Christian's thoughts and actions.

When and how should the conversation between the serpent and Eve have ended? The conversation should have ended with Eve's first response to the serpent: a statement of what God had said about the tree—end of dialogue!

Christ left us His example when the tempter (Satan) came to Him in the wilderness. Two times He simply answered the devil with the Word of God. The third time He started His statement with the words, *"Get thee hence, Satan: for it is written. . . ."* (Matthew 4:1-13). Jesus did not spend time having dialogue with evil spirits in whatever form they appeared. Likewise, He did not entertain the vain philosophies of men.

Guard Your Heart

Entertaining philosophies, concepts, ideas and opinions that do not agree with the Word of God is very destructive to a Christian and can affect the very heart of a man. Thoughts become actions, so dialogue carries a tremendous risk of consequences. The risk is greater because one's guard is down when dialogue is progressing. Dialogue on the surface appears to be innocuous, just an intellectual exchange of ideas or opinions. There are many scriptures that admonish us to guard what we hear and see and thereby protect ourselves spiritually from the evil influences of this world. Proverbs 4:23 records the following commandment: "Keep thy heart with all diligence; for out of it are the issues of life." The word "heart" used in this text refers to the feelings, intellect and will of man. The word "keep" means "to guard" (*Strong's Concordance*).

The power of dialogue is almost incomprehensible in its far-reaching effects. Approximately twenty-five years ago I was listening to a speaker, whose name I have long since forgotten; he made a statement, however, that I have never forgotten. He said that if people talk about absurd things long enough, those things will become the norm. I have observed this to be an accurate statement with regard to social norms in America. Many behaviors and lifestyles that are part of the present-day norms of the American culture were at one time considered to be abnormal, deviant or sinful behaviors. Yet, as those behaviors and lifestyles were talked about openly in the conversation format of dialogue, slowly but surely the abnormal became considered normal.

Another breeding ground for the eradication of the standards of moral behavior in America is the rebellion against the ultimate authority of God and His Word. While in college during the early 1970s I took a class called *Abnormal Psychology* and was surprised that the label of "abnormal behavior" was deemed appropriate for certain behaviors that the Bible clearly identified as "sinful." Over the years these same behaviors were reclassified and given other labels. Some were labeled as manifestations of a disease, and others were simply reclassified as normal. There is also a theory that some of these behaviors are genetic or hereditary in nature, though nature in itself clearly disproves this theory.

These ongoing reclassifications are indicative of the deteriorating morals of our nation and exemplify man's way of justifying his every inconsistency. Since the field of psychology does not acknowledge biblical absolutes with regard to the behavior of people, the reclassification of behaviors is considered to be an acceptable and intellectually sound practice.

The most detrimental result of sinful behavior being considered an illness or normal behavior is that individuals who are bound by sin and oppressed by Satan become deceived about the source of their problem. Likewise, they do not recognize their need for a remedy for their sinful state. These individuals may be experiencing tremendous emotional upheaval; yet, the remedy of repentance and liberation from sin by the power of Jesus Christ is, unfortunately, not a consideration in their minds.

Another consequential effect upon our society of the reclassification process is the endorsement by educators, even at the grade school level, that these sinful behaviors are acceptable or normal. Satan is striving to corrupt the minds of all people including children, the future of our country.

Satan understands the power and influence of communication and its everlasting consequences. According to James 3:5-6:

> Even so the tongue is a little member, and boasteth great things. Behold, how great a matter a little fire kindleth! And the tongue is a fire, a world of iniquity: so is the tongue among our members, that it defileth the whole body, and setteth on fire the course of nature; and it is set on fire of hell.

Satan's Dialogue

The objective of Satan's dialogue with man is always the same: to find a common ground where the seed of deception can be sown leading man into sin. Just as he did with Eve in the Garden of Eden, Satan would like to seduce

Christians to open their minds to entertain evil ideas, concepts and beliefs. Satan is working through any and every avenue he finds to promote his deluded, deceptive, and evil ideas. Christians' minds are the target of his agenda. We must be diligent in setting a guard at the door of our minds to prevent or reject information, ideas, concepts or beliefs that are not founded on scriptural truth.

Chapter Seven

The Lord Our Counselor

Christians understand that all humanity is engaged in a spiritual battle and the battlefield is in our minds. Thought patterns proceeding out of a carnal mind are governed by the senses; but the thought patterns of a spiritual mind are governed by biblical truth, faith and a trust in God. God's Word admonishes us to "Trust in the Lord with all thine heart; and lean not unto thine own understanding. In all thy ways acknowledge him, and he shall direct thy paths" (Proverbs 3:5-6).

Christians, when facing problems, trials, afflictions or circumstances in life, may be uncertain or even confused about which course of action would serve to resolve the problem. For this reason, an individual needs guidance or advice to know how to perceive a circumstance, make a decision and, if necessary, take action to resolve the dilemma. Jeremiah 10:23 portrays man's need for guidance as follows, ". . . [T]he way of man is not in himself: it is not in man that walketh to direct his steps." Whatever the reason for seeking counsel, the Bible tells us in Isaiah 9:6 that Jesus is our Counselor. According to *Strong's Concordance*, a counselor is one who guides and gives advice or counsel. Proverbs 8:14 also identifies the Lord as our counselor: "Counsel is mine, and sound wisdom: I am understanding; I have strength." Because of these attributes, the Lord desires that we seek counsel or guidance from Him. Psalm 73:24 not only tells us the Lord will guide us with His counsel, but explains that His counsel will lead us to glory.

The counsel of Jesus Christ is founded upon His knowledge of every facet that is involved in any given circumstance in our lives including past, present and future. He knows the end from the beginning of every trial we face. His counsel is based upon His love and pure intentions for our good. As we seek Him in prayer, He will guide our thoughts and our actions in dealing with or resolving every dilemma or circumstance. There are times when His wisdom will guide us to ". . . stand still and see the salvation of the Lord," as He will be the One to take the action (Exodus 14:13).

God has given us His Word and His Spirit to lead us into all truth and righteousness. The counsel of the Lord is "godly counsel." Psalm 1:1 states, "Blessed is the man that walketh not in the counsel of the ungodly. . . ." The ungodly being those who neither know God nor obey God's Word. Verse six of the same chapter states, "For the Lord knoweth the way of the righteous: but the way of the ungodly shall perish."

Walk Not in the Counsel of the Ungodly

An example is given in Isaiah chapters 30 and 31 of the Lord reproving Israel for seeking the counsel and help of Pharaoh and the Egyptians instead of God. These scriptural references clearly depict the shame, confusion and devastation that would come to Israel for their misplaced trust and allegiance:

> Woe to the rebellious children, saith the Lord, that take *counsel*, but not of me; and that cover with a covering, but not of my spirit, that they may add sin to sin: That walk to go down into Egypt, and *have not asked at my mouth*; to strengthen themselves in the strength of Pharaoh, and to trust in the shadow of Egypt! *Therefore shall the strength of Pharaoh be your shame, and the trust in the shadow of Egypt your confusion.* (Isaiah 30:1-3) (Italics mine)

> Woe to them that go down to Egypt for help; and stay on horses, and trust in chariots, because they are many; and in horsemen, because they are very strong; *but they look not unto the Holy One of Israel, neither seek the Lord!* Yet he also is wise, and will bring evil, and will not call back his words: but will arise against the house of the evildoers, and against the help of them that work iniquity. Now the Egyptians are men, and not God; and their horses flesh and not spirit. When the Lord shall stretch out his hand, both he that helpeth shall fall, and he that is holpen [helped] shall fall down, and they all shall fail together. (Isaiah 31:1-3) (Italics mine)

The children of Israel were considered rebellious because they did not rely on God for guidance or counsel, nor did they depend on Him as their source of deliverance and help. They sought counsel from and allegiance with Pharaoh and trusted in the strength of Egypt. Christians might judge the nation of Israel and criticize her for not trusting in God. Yet we, the spiritual seed of Abraham, often make the same mistake. How frequently we turn to the wisdom of men to find the answers to our problems in life, forgetting that God is the author and finisher of our faith. He knows the end from the beginning of all life's circumstances, and with every problem He gives us this promise:

> Likewise the Spirit also helpeth our infirmities: for we know not what we should pray for as we ought: but the Spirit itself maketh intercession for us with groanings which cannot be uttered. And he that searcheth the hearts knoweth what is the mind of the Spirit, because he maketh intercession for the saints according to the will of God. And we know that all things work together for good to them that love God, to them who are the called according to his purpose. For whom he did foreknow, he also did predestinate to be conformed to the image of his Son, that he might be the firstborn among many brethren. Moreover whom he did predestinate, them he also called: and whom he called, them he also justified: and whom he justified, them he also glorified. What shall we then say to these things? If God be for us, who can be against us? (Romans 8:26-31)

Godly Counsel

As Christians, our first source of guidance should always come through prayer and the Word of God. Prayer will shed light on and dispel the confusion in our minds. God will speak to our hearts giving us direction for our thoughts and actions.

As we pray, often the Holy Ghost will intercede for us and through us, bringing peace and comfort in the midst of our trouble. If God's hand of providence is allowing and leading us through a difficult circumstance, then we shall come forth as gold (Job 23:10). If we are facing an attack of our adversary, ultimately, he will be defeated, and we will be victorious.

A second source of godly counsel comes to a Christian through the preaching of the Word of God. After prayerfully seeking God for an answer to a problem, frequently a sermon will be preached giving us understanding and clear direction to resolve the problem or to wait on God for resolution. God's counsel may also be channeled through a pastor or another child of God. The important point to remember is that God is our counselor and He will answer our prayers and supply our needs if we will but ask Him.

> Ask, and it shall be given you; seek, and ye shall find; knock, and it shall be opened unto you: For every one that asketh receiveth; and he that seeketh findeth; and to him that knocketh it shall be opened. (Matthew 7:7-8)

> If any of you lack wisdom, let him ask of God, that giveth to all men liberally, and

upbraideth not; and it shall be given him.
(James 1:5)

Just as the Israelites were not to look to Pharaoh or
Egypt for counsel and help, Christians should not trust in
the wisdom or counsel of man or the systems of this world.
Paul expounded on this truth to the Corinthian church in
the following text:

> And I, brethren, when I came to you, came
> not with the excellency of speech or of
> wisdom, declaring unto you the testimony of
> God. For I determined not to know anything
> among you, save Jesus Christ, and him
> crucified. And I was with you in weakness,
> and in fear, and in much trembling. And my
> speech and my preaching was not with
> enticing words of man's wisdom, but in
> demonstration of the Spirit and of power:
> *That your faith should not stand in the
> wisdom of men, but in the power of God.*
> (I Corinthians 2:1-5) (Italics are mine)

With the understanding that our faith should not stand
in the wisdom of men, let me pose a question. Would a
child of God prosper from counsel that arises from the
wisdom of men who possess only a carnal mind and
nature? In a letter to the saints at Corinth, Paul depicted the
contrast between the thoughts and comprehension of a
spiritual man, one who has received the Holy Ghost, and a
natural [carnal] man who has not received the Spirit of
God:

Now we have received, not the spirit of the world, but the spirit which is of God; that we might know the things that are freely given to us of God. Which things also we speak, not in the words which man's wisdom teacheth, but which the Holy Ghost teacheth; comparing spiritual things with spiritual. *But the natural man receiveth not the things of the Spirit of God: for they are foolishness unto him: neither can he know them, because they are spiritually discerned.* But he that is spiritual judgeth all things, yet he himself is judged of no man. For who hath known the mind of the Lord, that he may instruct him? *But we have the mind of Christ.* (I Corinthians 2:12-16) (Italics mine)

The preceding scriptures clearly indicate that a natural man, a man who does not have the Spirit of God, cannot comprehend the things of the Spirit. Consider again this question: Would it be wise for a Holy Ghost-filled person to seek counsel from an individual who does not have the Holy Ghost? Does that person understand or could he give sound advice regarding spiritual battles? After receiving the Holy Spirit, Christians are given the power to be transformed by the renewing of their minds in order that they would not be conformed to this world (Romans 12:2). The "adversary" will come against a child of God attempting to bring him back into captivity and into carnal reasoning, resulting not only in confusion, but also in fear, doubt and temptation.

Satan, who transforms himself into an angel of light (II Corinthians 11:14), wants to seduce Christians to rely on their own or another man's wisdom and strength; if he succeeds they will reap the same shame, confusion and destruction that Israel reaped.

As Paul wrote in his letter to the Galatians in 3:3, "Are ye so foolish? having begun in the Spirit, are ye now made perfect by the flesh?" Consider for a moment this scripture within the context of our Christian life. If a child of God is struggling with emotions of sadness, despair, doubt, anxiety, confusion or any other of the multitude of emotions brought on by the trials of life or the buffeting of our adversary, how could a secular counselor, whatever his education, help this individual? To whom did Paul turn when he was experiencing great suffering and despair? Paul related the following experience to the saints at Corinth in his second epistle:

> Blessed be God, even the Father of our Lord Jesus Christ, the Father of mercies, and the God of all comfort; *Who comforteth us in all our tribulation, that we may be able to comfort them which are in any trouble,* by the comfort wherewith we ourselves are comforted of God. For as the sufferings of Christ abound in us, so our consolation also aboundeth by Christ. And whether we be afflicted, it is for your consolation and salvation, which is effectual in the enduring of the same sufferings which we also suffer: or whether we be comforted, it is for your consolation and salvation. And our hope of you is stedfast, knowing, that as ye are partakers of the sufferings, so shall ye be also of the consolation. For we would not,

brethren, have you ignorant of our trouble which came to us in Asia, that we were pressed out of measure, above strength, insomuch that we despaired even of life: But we had the sentence of death in ourselves, *that we should not trust in ourselves, but in God which raiseth the dead:* Who delivered us from so great a death, and doth deliver: in whom we trust that he will yet deliver us. (II Corinthians 1:3-10) (Italics mine)

The consideration is not one of whether it is right or wrong to go to a psychiatrist, social worker or therapist; rather, through what source does godly counsel come to a child of God for the trouble he encounters in his life? We need to consider again the promise of God: "God is our refuge and strength, a very present help in trouble. Therefore will not we fear, though the earth be removed, and though the mountains be carried into the midst of the sea" (Psalm 46:1-2).

Christians must cautiously consider whether the counsel they seek is godly or ungodly. In addition, they need to understand the difference between a scriptural perspective of counseling and a secular perspective of counseling.

Chapter Eight

Godly Counsel Versus Secular Counsel

Secular counselors, whether mental health professionals, social workers or nurses, all use fundamental principles of psychology and psychiatry as the basis for their assessments and interventions with clients. They defer to the client's psychiatrist as the ultimate authority with regard to the medical plan of treatment. Understanding the dynamics of counseling as related to secular systems requires a closer look at some of the techniques used in psychotherapy.

Psychiatry is defined as "a branch of medicine that deals with mental, emotional, or behavioral disorders." According to *Synopsis*, "The problems that take people to psychiatrists for treatment are of two kinds: those that seem to have their origins largely in the remote past of patients' lives and those that seem to arise largely from current stresses and pressures that seem beyond the patients' conscious control" (Kaplan 824). The choice of psychotherapy is based on whether the patients' problems were mainly from past or current experiences. If stemming from the past, psychoanalysis would be the therapy of choice. If the patients' emotional problems arise from more current stress factors, psychoanalytic therapy would be indicated (Kaplan 824). Following is a brief description of these two types of therapy contrasted with scriptural truth dealing with the same subject matter.

Psychoanalysis

Psychoanalysis consists of encouraging the patient to bring to the conscious mind repressed experiences, particularly experiences that are painful or negative, and the related thoughts, feelings and fantasies associated with those experiences. The authors of *Synopsis* referred to these repressed negative experiences as "noxious psychic material" (Kaplan 825-826). The patient is to verbalize all his memories or thoughts, without selection, to the therapist through "free association." In free association the patient is instructed to "say everything that comes to mind without any censoring, regardless of whether they believe the thought to be unacceptable, unimportant, or embarrassing" (Kaplan 826).

Transference, another aspect of psychoanalysis, involves the patient expressing feelings toward the therapist, whether negative or positive, that he may have felt toward his parents or other parental figures from his past. An expression of negative transference, even if done in a highly labile and volatile manner, is not discouraged (Kaplan 826).

Synopsis identifies the role of the analyst as preparing the patient to deal with anxiety-producing thoughts that are uncovered, increasing the patient's awareness of the natural tendency to resist thoughts that are painful and helping the individual piece together the experiences of his past. The analyst also attempts to interpret the patient's associations in hopes of facilitating an understanding of the patient's current emotional conflicts and the historical factors that influenced him. Finally, the analyst attempts to help the patient gain true insights into relationships based on mature and realistic expectations (Kaplan 825-827).

The authors of *Synopsis* explained that the average duration of treatment is three to six years, four or more times per week with sessions lasting 45 to 50 minutes. The authors also identified several circumstances that are viewed as contraindications for psychoanalysis including the following:

- In general, young adults are considered to be the ideal candidates for psychoanalysis. Apparently, for older adults, most analysts view the success of psychoanalysis as being dependent upon the individuals desire for change as well as his capacity for thoughtful introspection.
- Psychoanalysis could be detrimental if the patient's life circumstances are not likely to change or to be modified in some way.
- The dynamics of the patient-therapist relationship are sometimes considered a contraindication to psychoanalysis as "[s]ome patients work better with some analysts than with others."
- Individuals with antisocial personality disorder are usually not considered good candidates for psychoanalysis related to their inability to develop emotional attachments with others and their tendency to exhibit cruel behavior toward others with no remorse.

- Time constraints: as was stated previously, psychoanalysis usually lasts between three to six years and often individuals in hope of change are not able to participate for these extended periods of time. (Kaplan 827-828).

Understanding the Will of the Lord

How does a scriptural perspective of counseling differ conceptually from the secular counseling model involved in psychoanalysis? Christians are to be led by the Spirit of God and not by the flesh. According to Ephesians 5:15-17 Christians are to ". . . walk circumspectly, not as fools, but as wise. Redeeming the time, because the days are evil. Wherefore be ye not unwise, but understanding what the will of the Lord is." To walk circumspectly means, "to look around, be cautious," [and] "careful to consider all circumstances and possible consequences." In light of the preceding scriptures, Christians need to cautiously evaluate the basic elements of psychoanalysis before participating in this type of therapy.

Christians must carefully consider what has been identified as the "fundamental rule of psychoanalysis," which is that patients must agree to tell the analyst anything that comes to their minds without censoring (Kaplan 826). Many scriptures in the Bible admonish a Christian to be discrete in his conversations. In addition, many scriptures reveal the possible effect that our words can have not only on ourselves but also on others. Consider the following scriptures:

A fool uttereth all his mind: but a wise man keepeth it in till afterwards.

94

Even a fool, when he holdeth his peace, is counted wise: and he that shutteth his lips is esteemed a man of understanding.

The tongue of the wise useth knowledge aright: but the mouth of fools poureth out foolishness.

A wholesome tongue is a tree of life: but perverseness therein is a breach in the spirit. (Proverbs 29:11; 17:28; 15:2; 4)

Wherefore, my beloved brethren, let every man be swift to hear, slow to speak, slow to wrath: For the wrath of man worketh not the righteousness of God.

Even so the tongue is a little member, and boasteth great things. Behold, how great a matter a little fire kindleth! And the tongue is a fire, a world of iniquity: so is the tongue among our members, that it defileth the whole body, and setteth on fire the course of nature; and it is set on fire of hell.

Who is a wise man and endued with knowledge among you? let him show out of a good conversation [behavior: actions and words] his works with meekness of wisdom. (James 1:19-20 and 3:5-6; 13)

The Lord is teaching us to be careful what we speak. The scriptures portray the power of the spoken word and its ability to bring destruction not only to others but also to ourselves. When an individual repeatedly thinks and speaks of painful or negative experiences and the trauma these experiences have caused him, he is developing habitual thought patterns of a negative or destructive nature that will become "strongholds" in his mind (Chapter 5, page 55).

The authors of *Synopsis* were correct in having referred to the repressed negative thoughts as *noxious psychic material* because by definition noxious means "constituting a harmful influence on the mind or behavior." Repeatedly discussing the negative experiences that occurred in our past will result in a harmful influence on our minds and our behavior. One of the examples that *Webster's Dictionary* gives as a use of the word noxious is that noxious "wastes turn our steams into sewers." The Holy Ghost is described as a river of living water (John 7:38-39). It would be tragic to contaminate this pure river with noxious wastes (memories) from our past or the present. Forgiveness keeps this river clean.

Individuals who have been involved in psychoanalysis often develop a pattern of talking continually about themselves and their painful life experiences. Their focus is predominantly inward and negative, producing a demeanor and aura around them that repels and alienates them from other people. And, their repetitive behavior of discussing their painful experiences is not usually restricted to their counseling sessions with their therapists or counselors. After engaging in a few conversations with such individuals, others will avoid them, not wanting to hear again their repertoire of woes (noxious psychic material).

A Sound Mind is a Disciplined Mind

As mentioned previously, during the technique of free association the analyst encourages the individual to allow his thoughts to run unguarded with the purpose of bringing to the conscious mind painful memories of past experiences. The analyst attempts to prepare the patient for the anxiety he may feel as these memories flood his mind. In contrast to this purposeful activity of resurrecting noxious, anxiety-provoking memories, the Lord instructs us to discipline our minds to think on things that are good or wholesome, which is defined as "promoting health or well-being of mind or spirit."

> Finally, brethren whatsoever things are true, whatsoever things are honest, whatsoever things are just, whatsoever things are pure, whatsoever things are lovely, whatsoever things are of good report; if there be any virtue, and if there be any praise, think on these things. (Philippians 4:7)

In the event that anxiety-provoking thoughts or memories do come to mind, the Lord also instructs His children how they are to respond to these thoughts and the feelings of anxiety.

> Be *careful* [defined by *Strong's Concordance* as *anxious*] for nothing; but in every thing by prayer and supplication with thanksgiving let your requests be made known unto God. And the peace of God, which passeth all understanding, shall keep your hearts and minds through Christ Jesus. (Philippians 4:6) (Italics mine)

Clearly, Jesus is directing Christians to not be anxious about anything but to bring every circumstance to Him in prayer with thanksgiving, and He will give them the peace of God, which will keep or guard their minds.

Another scripture compelling Christians to discipline their minds is I Peter 1:13: "Gird up the loins of your mind. . . ." We are to discipline our minds to think spiritually, for as a man thinketh in his heart so is he (Proverbs 23:7). Allowing our minds to run rampant and unguarded, especially with negative, painful thoughts, will eventually cause both mental and emotional instability, producing a vulnerability to satanic oppression. Christians are to raise a shield of faith in order to quench all the fiery darts of the wicked that come in the form of negative or evil thoughts (Ephesians 6:16).

Finally, in addressing the list of contraindications to psychoanalysis, it is noteworthy that there are no contraindications for God's intervention in an individual's life regardless of his age or his mental or emotional problems. Secondly, there are many life circumstances that cannot be altered by man's intervention; however, in Matthew 19:26 Jesus said, "With men this is impossible; but **with God all things are possible**." Every obstacle becomes an opportunity for a miracle in the hands of God whether it be changing people's thinking, behaviors, character or their circumstances. For example, the man spoken of in chapter one of this book, who was possessed with devils and who would probably have been misdiagnosed as having antisocial personality disorder, would not have been considered a good candidate for psychoanalysis. His psychological and spiritual problems would have met more than one of the criteria for eliminating the choice of psychoanalysis as part of his treatment plan. His violent and self-destructive behaviors would no doubt have brought about conflicts between him and the analyst—if the man could have been restrained long enough for a few minutes of analysis. Yet, after a very brief encounter with Jesus, the demoniac from Gadara was instantaneously delivered and subsequently declared to be in his "right mind" (4-6).

Psychoanalytic Psychotherapy

The second type of therapy is psychoanalytic psychotherapy, which focuses on patients' current conflicts within themselves and in relationships with other people. The duration of therapy may range from one session to many years of treatment with a frequency of interviews as often as one to three per week. Some of the types of psychotherapeutic interventions that are used for both insight-oriented and supportive psychotherapy include: interpretation, confrontation, clarification, encouragement to elaborate, empathetic validation, advice and praise and affirmation. [These interventions need no further explanation as they are self-explanatory and are part of the dynamics of most types of communication]. The therapist is attempting to assist patients in gaining insights into their psychological functioning and personality while supporting them in this process. The therapist is also attempting to elicit more appropriate or adaptive patterns of behavior along with a more stable emotional status (Kaplan 828-830).

The Source of all Conflicts

The focus of psychoanalytic therapy is on conflicts in interpersonal relationships as well as an individual's conflicts within himself. The Bible contains a wealth of knowledge regarding relationships not only in the natural realm but also in the spiritual. In Luke 6:27-28 Jesus tells us to do the following: ". . . Love your enemies, do good to them which hate you, Bless them that curse you, and pray for them which despitefully use you." And according to Matthew 7:12, we are instructed to treat other individuals as we would want to be treated, "Therefore all things whatsoever ye would that men should do to you, do ye even so to them: for this is the law and the prophets."

The Word of God clarifies the truth about man's carnal or sinful nature, which is the source of all conflicts, whether internal or in relationships with other individuals. However, the most important relationship conflict that exists for mankind is his separation from God. When this conflict is resolved through repentance, remission of sins and receiving the Holy Spirit, man then has the ability through Christ to resolve both the conflicts within himself and those he has with other people. The truth is that man is not able to become righteous without the help of God; therefore, without God in his life, he will experience difficulty in resolving his own inner conflicts and those conflicts he has with others.

Having the Holy Spirit and living by the Word of God will yield the peaceable fruit of righteousness. God has promised us that "When a man's ways please the Lord, he maketh even his enemies to be at peace with him" (Proverbs 16:7). Whatever emotional wounds we have sustained in life will be healed by His love if we allow Him to work in our hearts.

I am reminded of a testimony concerning my oldest son, Joshua, who by the age of 14 had suffered years of painful emotional experiences leaving him critically wounded in his spirit. These wounds precipitated a variety of negative behaviors including bitterness, anger and rebellion. He was attending a Christian school and a conference was scheduled with the principal, pastor, my son and me. As the conference began, the principal referred to a long list he had written of my son's unacceptable behaviors in school and the attempts that had been made to resolve these behavior problems. I anticipated that the outcome of this conference might lead to him being expelled from school, but that was not my foremost concern during the conference.

My greatest concern was the portrayal of hopelessness that was being presented regarding the subject of my son being able or willing to change his behavior. **With God there is always hope and nothing is impossible**. I made the request that Josh leave the room and my request was quickly granted. I explained to the principal and pastor that there were years of hurt and scars in my son's life and that despite all seeming futility of the attempts that had already been made, we needed to keep trying. As I desperately tried to persuade them, I felt the unction of the Holy Ghost and spoke with faith as I said, *"God is going to do something for my son."* Being led by the Spirit, we began to pray. As we prayed together, the Spirit made intercession and our petitions were heard. The conference ended with a resolve that Josh would remain in the school and that efforts would continue to be made to help him. Two weeks later he received the Holy Ghost, and God did for him what no counselor could ever do.

On the night Josh received the Holy Ghost, he prayed fervently for a long period of time and then began to weep. His face revealed emotional pain and anguish. He began speaking with other tongues as he was filled with the Holy Spirit, but still continued to weep. Usually, the experience of receiving the Holy Ghost is accompanied by an expression of joy, but he continued to weep for quite some time. Our pastor walked behind him and put his arms around him. As soon as the pastor embraced Josh he also began to weep and there was a similar expression of anguish on his face. As I stood watching, my heart ached, and confusion filled my mind. In my mind I questioned, *Lord what is happening?* To my mind came this immediate response: *I am healing his wounds.*

Josh may very well have grown up an angry and bitter man had not God intervened in his life. Josh completed all of his education and went on to graduate from Indiana Bible College. Today, he is a preacher of the gospel and the youth pastor at Calvary Tabernacle in Indianapolis. Years of psychotherapy could not have accomplished what God did in that one church service. However, if my son had not cried out to God, the miracle would never have taken place. Christians must realize that **Jesus is always the answer** and turn to Him for their deliverance and healing.

God's Counsel Versus Secular Counsel

Christians are not exempt from conflicts and difficulties in life. As discussed in the previous chapter, the Lord wants to be our counselor and to guide us through all of life's circumstances. He does not want His children to be guided by the carnal mind of man or to rely on human ability. We are to trust in Him and not in our own wisdom or knowledge, and to acknowledge Him through prayer; then, He will direct our paths—our lives (Proverbs 3:5-6).

People who do not have a relationship with God have no other alternative than to rely on their own or another man's wisdom. Such dependence, however, really only contributes to their downfall because of the inability of man to help himself in the area of the spiritual battles he encounters. What man needs to recognize is his utterly helpless state without God. Once he realizes his need for God and obeys His Word, he will begin to understand that there is no problem that God cannot take care of, no need that He cannot meet.

During difficult times, we need to pray and seek God for the answer to our problems; however, we may also request others in the church to pray with us and for us. We may be led by the Spirit to talk to someone in the church about what we are experiencing. Sharing this information often brings enough clarity to our perceptions to help us recognize how God is already directing us regarding the problem. The anticipated result from an encounter or discussion with the pastor, elder or a mature child of God is that you will receive the Lord's counsel as channeled through one of His anointed vessels.

As children of God, we need to be sensitive to the voice of the Lord and to minister to others, allowing ourselves to be used as a vessel through which God's counsel is channeled. We cannot expect the pastor to be the only one who ministers to emotionally hurting individuals. Initially, their need for support may be very great until they become more disciplined in their thinking and more knowledgeable in the Word of God. Newborn Christians do not yet know how to rightly divide the Word of God and have not developed a sensitivity to the leading of the Spirit of God. As the body of Christ, we will not be able to meet the needs of the world unless we are sensitive to the voice of God and knowledgeable about His Word. Every person who received the gift of the Holy Ghost has access to God's wisdom and knowledge for we have the mind of Christ in us.

Anyone believing that a child of God must have a counseling degree to minister to certain individuals is sadly mistaken. The Word of God declares:

> Verily, verily, I say unto you, He that believeth on me, the works that I do shall he do also; and greater works than these shall he do; because I go unto my Father. And whatsoever ye shall ask in my name, that will I do, that the Father may be glorified in the Son. If ye shall ask any thing in my name, I will do it. (John 14:12-14)

If Satan could deceive the church into believing that it would take a secular education or a college degree to be of help to people with emotional problems, then our ability to reach most lost souls would be undermined. Likewise, limiting the ministry of helping emotionally crippled individuals to only those in the church who are credentialed counselors is a gross error. A mature, spirit-filled saint should be able to guide hurting individuals to the knowledge of the truth of deliverance and emotional healing, which is *free* to anyone who asks. According to II Corinthians 1:3-4:

> Blessed be God, even the Father of our Lord Jesus Christ, the Father of mercies, and the God of all comfort; Who comforteth us in all our tribulation, that we may be able to comfort them which are in *any trouble*, by the

comfort wherewith we ourselves are comforted of God. (Italics mine)

The body of Christ must purge from the church the leaven of the vain philosophies of the world. We need to use the discernment God has given us to defeat the seducing spirits and doctrines of devils that will arise in an attempt to cause people to depart from the faith. Incorporating the world's philosophy into the church limits God because His ways are perfect and Holy and He will not yield to the corruption of man's vain devices. Jesus has sent us forth to proclaim "Him" and to minister to the world, preaching the gospel of Christ that will heal the brokenhearted, deliver the captives, give sight to the blind and set at liberty all those that are bruised or emotionally hurting (Luke 4:18).

What a child of God needs from his brethren, whether it be his pastor, teacher or fellow saint, **is to be assured that God is a very present help in the time of trouble** (Psalm 46:1). He may even need to be reminded that the Word of God and Spirit of God in him give him the ability to be more than a conqueror through Christ who loves him. He must believe that nothing can separate him from the love of God (Romans 8:37-39). As Christians we are able through the Spirit of God and with the Word of God to encourage those that are hurting emotionally. We are also able to lift them up in prayer and to intercede on their behalf.

In summary, godly counsel may be obtained in any or all of the following ways:

- Praying and seeking God for His counsel and direction

- Attending church where the anointed preaching will provide God's counsel and direction
- Consistent Bible reading and study combined with prayer for guidance from God
- Praying steadfastly, *waiting* on God to reveal His plan
- Talking to the pastor, an elder or another child of God who as a yielded vessel might guide or advise us with the Word of God or serve as a channel for God's Spirit to work through

There are many other ways that a Christian may receive God's counsel and direction, but these are the most common. The most difficult aspect of the practice of seeking God's counsel is that He does not always provide the answer that we have predetermined to be best for us and He does not always answer within our time frame. Our self-will and impatience may foolishly cause us to seek an alternative and more immediate answer. Satan capitalizes on a Christian's self-will and impatience with the offer of his immediate solutions to the problem. However, these quick-fix remedies often result in long-term problems.

Chapter Nine

A Quick-Fix Remedy

As a master of deceit, Satan has created the ever-present illusion that there is a quick-fix remedy for the problems and circumstances encountered in everyday life. Our belief that man should have immediate gratification of his needs and that he should have to experience *neither want nor suffering* reinforces Satan's illusion. The quick and easy remedies for life's problems are immediate in nature, but the end result is usually not what was anticipated. Satan would like Christians to continually react to the circumstances of life through their carnal mind and emotions rather than their spiritual mind and faith.

If you have a headache, take Tylenol. For your financial problems, secure a loan. Charge the new clothes you want for the upcoming event. If you are sick, call the doctor. Feeling discouraged or depressed—make an appointment with a psychiatrist or a counselor. When you are lonely, try the Internet. These solutions are often transient in nature and may not truly solve the problem though they are immediately accessible. Christians, if not careful, may unwisely resort to the systems and remedies of the world instead of looking to Christ to supply all of their needs "according to his riches in glory" (Philippians 4:19).

Satan knows that if he can keep Christians on a carnal plane he will have a degree of influence and power over them because he is ". . . the prince of this world" (John 12:31). Regarding afflictions and sicknesses, the Word of God instructs us as follows:

> Is any among you afflicted? let him pray. Is any merry? let him sing psalms. Is any sick among you? let him call for the elders of the church; and let them pray over him, anointing him with oil in the name of the Lord: And the prayer of faith shall save the sick and the Lord shall raise him up; and if he have committed sins, they shall be forgiven him. Confess your faults one to another, and pray one for another, that ye may be healed. The effectual fervent prayer of a righteous man availeth much. Elias was a man subject to like passions as we are, and he prayed earnestly that it might not rain: and it rained not on the earth by the space of three years and six months. And he prayed again, and the heaven gave rain, and the earth brought forth her fruit. (James 5:13-18)

God has given Christians a remedy for sicknesses and afflictions, but frequently we are more accustomed to meeting these needs through the world's remedies—that is, until the problem gets too big for the solutions or cures of this world. If the headache is diagnosed as inoperable brain cancer, then we run to the "Master Physician." When our charge cards are maxed out at 21% interest, and the bank denies us a loan, then we go to Jesus.

What was previously considered just another option now becomes clearly the only option as we fervently pray for God to intervene. Yet, we are skeptical that God will answer because our heart condemns us (I John 3:20). God has been factored out or put on a shelf, so how can we go to Him now for our needs? Nevertheless, with everlasting mercy He hears our cry for help, and intervenes, because He is ". . . greater than our heart, and knoweth all things" (I John 3:20). With the crisis under control, we breathe a prayer of thankfulness and determine to put our trust in God and not to neglect our precious relationship with Him.

Before long, however, we may again turn our confidence toward worldly systems and solutions when problems arise, if we have not learned to rely on Jesus and His promises in our everyday life. Christians need to practice the scripture that commands us to, ". . . seek ye first the kingdom of God, and his righteousness; and all these things shall be added unto you" (Matthew 6:33).

The prayer lives of many Christians are sporadic and for others almost nonexistent, which defeats the practice of using their faith. Is it any wonder that God asks, ". . . Nevertheless when the Son of man cometh, shall he find faith on the earth?" (Luke 18:8). Romans 12:3 informs us that God has given to every man a measure of faith. If one's faith is not practiced, the lack of discipline will lead to "little faith" and a spiritual state of doubt and unbelief, often resulting in a compromised allegiance with the world.

Christians who attempt to live by both the world's philosophy and a scriptural philosophy of life will find themselves in a state of utter confusion. This divided allegiance makes it difficult to trust Jesus with their problems. God will and does provide for His children's needs. However, Christians must choose to follow His commandments concerning how to receive the help needed from Him. Faith in God will stand against the carnal reasoning and lifestyles that the world and Satan would like to impose upon us.

The society in which we live promotes the philosophy that we should not have to suffer pain, sorrow, need or hardship, all of which produce a degree of emotional discomfort. However, emotional suffering many times results in changes in our thinking and behavior that are beneficial. If emotional discomfort is labeled as abnormal, detrimental or undesirable, we will not benefit from the experience. Probably the most beneficial result of going through the hardships of life is that these experiences can cause us to take a more serious and realistic look at life and ourselves and subsequently discover our need for God and our need for repentance. The world's solutions for life's hardships are imitations of God's true remedy. Every source of media in our society today promotes prescription medications as the solution for emotional suffering. Psychotropic drugs usually only mask the symptoms of the underlying problems. This quick-fix remedy, which affords at best only partial relief, if any, is temporary in nature and serves to undermine the awareness and actions that might have been taken by the individual to find the true remedy. The widespread use of psychotropics in our society is further evidence of the emotionally crippled state of the citizens of our nation.

Pharmaceutical companies scramble to market their drugs, while anticipating neither healing nor cure for the individuals being treated with the drugs, expecting rather, a greater dependence on them. The consistent reinforcement through means of the media and advertisements to seek immediate relief from negative emotions often dictates our reactions to these emotions; a rejection of the alternative view that negative emotions can serve as an impetus for the positive changes needed in our lives.

Chapter Ten

Biological Psychiatry

As was discussed previously, the authors of *Synopsis* believe that the research data from the last two decades supports the theory that every psychiatric disorder has a biological component (Kaplan 25-26). Belief in this theory has dramatically changed the treatment protocol for mental disorders. One of the most significant changes is that psychiatric drugs have become the "popular" method of treatment for mental disorders almost to the exclusion of other therapies. Frequently, psychiatric drugs are prescribed by physicians without any consideration or assessment of any other underlying physical causes such as "hypothyroidism, estrogen deficiency, or head injury" (Breggin 6). Likewise, psychosocial factors contributing to emotional problems are de-emphasized, though according to Dr. Breggin, ". . . most people with depression and anxiety have obvious reasons for how they feel. These reasons are often apparent in their everyday lives. . ." (7). Yet, the emphasis regarding the causes and treatment of mental disorders is primarily focused on a biological component. Psychiatrists and theoreticians acknowledge, but downplay, the psychosocial factors that influence an individual's emotional state.

Unfortunately, our society desires a quick-fix remedy for mental disorders and, therefore, readily accepts the theory that mental disorders are caused by biochemical imbalances in the brain which could be remedied simply by taking a pill. Acceptance of this quick-fix solution is preferable to the alternative: the arduous task of identifying and working toward resolution of emotional problems that are related to ". . .conflicts in the home, at work, or in society, painful life experiences, confused values, a lack of direction, or other aspects of human life" (Breggin 6).

Hypothetical Causes of Psychiatric Disorders

The authors of *Synopsis* in discussing the cause of generalized anxiety disorder made the following statement: "As with most mental disorders, the cause of generalized anxiety disorder is not known." Causative models for most psychiatric disorders involve theories associated with biological, psychosocial and genetic factors (Kaplan 612-613).

The verdict is basically the same for substance-related disorders. According to *Synopsis,* ". . . substance abuse and substance dependence are caused by a person's taking a particular substance in an abusive pattern." Since this explanation of cause is really only a description of the behavior, the authors indicated that there are multiple theories for the causal basis of this disorder again within the realm of biological, psychosocial and genetic factors (Kaplan 390-392).

With regard to schizophrenia the following statement was made: "The cause of schizophrenia is not known" (Kaplan 463). Psychosocial, genetic and biological factors are implicated with multiple theories and corresponding

114

explanations about how these factors may influence the onset of this disorder (Kaplan 463-470). The theories, however, are as inconclusive as the data from the research used in support of the theories. For example, in discussing the possibility of a genetic influence in the development of schizophrenia, the following statement was made:

> Genetic studies clearly *suggest* that schizophrenia is an illness with a biological substrate. Nevertheless, studies of monozygotic twins repeatedly show that environmental and psychological factors have some importance in the development of schizophrenia, *since many twins are discordant for the illness.* (Kaplan 469) (Italics mine)

The preceding statement implied that there are studies suggestive of genetics as a cause in schizophrenia, yet studies with identical twins do not support this theory. How valid are the hypothetical causes of psychiatric disorders if they are based on inconclusive research?

Likewise, within the category of mood disorders (major depressive disorder and Bipolar I disorder) there are impediments to identifying the causes of these disorders:

> *The causal basis for mood disorders is not known. The many attempts to identify a biological or psychosocial cause of mood disorders* may have been hampered by the heterogeneity of the patient population that is defined by any of the available, clinically based diagnostic systems, including DSM-IV.

The causative factors can artificially be divided into biological factors, genetic factors, and psychosocial factors. That division is artificial because of the likelihood that the three realms interact among themselves. (Kaplan 518) (Italics mine)

The authors of *Synopsis* have stated that they do not know the cause of mood disorders and are not sure of the interrelationship among the factors they identify as being causal. Research is hampered due to the heterogeneity [diversity; dissimilarity] of the patient population. Not only is there diversity in the individuals' environments, there is likewise an individuality variable that will never be reconciled because God has made every human being a unique and different entity. Identical twins, though raised by the same parents in the same home and attending the same schools, will become different in their personalities and psychosocial makeup.

In what appears to be an attempt to circumvent the "absolute" of God-given, individual uniqueness, and to diminish the importance of environmental and psychosocial factors, psychiatrists and researchers have turned to experiments using animal models to gain support for their theory of a biological component as the dominant factor in the psychopathology of humans.

Animal Models of Research

The use of animal models in research to identify the psychopathology of the human mind seems illogical. There are major differences between the animal and human mind: intellectual capability, reasoning ability, memory and emotional makeup, just to mention a few. The following example of animal research from which researchers inferred support for biological psychiatry, was based on having produced by pharmacological means, behavioral abnormalities in animals analogous to the paranoid psychotic behaviors of schizophrenics:

> . . . [A]nimals given amphetamines acted in a stereotyped, inappropriately aggressive, and apparently frightened manner that was similar to paranoid psychotic symptoms in humans. (Kaplan 181)

The significance of amphetamines causing aggressive and fearful behavior in animals is related to the dopamine hypothesis of schizophrenia. "Amphetamine causes the release of dopamine . . . [t]hus, increasing the amount of dopamine present in the synapse," the space between nerve cells (Kaplan 137). Since the behavior of the animals was *believed to be similar* to paranoid psychotic symptoms in humans, theoretically it could be assumed that individuals with these symptoms may be suffering from an increased amount of dopamine in the synapses—thus, rendering hypothetical support to the theory of biological psychiatry.

Nevertheless, the only definite conclusion that could be drawn from this experiment is that the amphetamines caused some type of brain dysfunction that resulted in mental and behavioral changes in the animals. This is true whether the drug is given to animals or humans. According to the authors of *Synopsis,* amphetamine "can, when given in high enough doses, induce psychotic symptoms in nonschizophrenic persons" (Kaplan 138).

The authors of *Synopsis* admitted that with regard to this experiment and another one similar to it that "Both. . . models are thought to be too simplistic in their concepts of cause, but they remain as early paradigms for that type of research" (Kaplan 181).

Christians recognize that there are other significant differences between animals and humans. Animals are not the objects of the spiritual battle of evil trying to defeat good. Though Satan cannot defeat God, he is vehemently trying to bring destruction and eternal damnation to God's beloved mankind. Men, not animals, are the target of Satan's attack and deception. Also, animals cannot partake of the life-transforming experience of receiving the Spirit of God within them. As was discussed in chapter four, researchers disregard the spiritual realm as a factor in the cause of mental disorders, which only contributes to the fallacy surrounding the theories and treatment of psychiatric disorders.

The previous information substantiates the existence of a significant knowledge deficit regarding the causes of most psychiatric disorders. Therefore, if the cause of a mental disorder is not known and is thought to be attributed to multiple factors, biological, psychosocial and genetic, then the treatment would most likely require a variety of intervention techniques to effect a positive response. This is usually not the case since, more often than not, psychotropics are prescribed without other supporting therapies such as psychotherapy, counseling or even participation in a support group. Jeffrey Kluger explained in an article in the November 3, 2003 issue of *TIME* magazine entitled, "Medicating Young Minds" that part of the reason for the lack of supporting therapies is the difficulty of receiving reimbursement for those services through the patient's insurance company (55). However, I believe the main factor influencing the lack of supporting therapies is based on the *speculation* that mental disorders are a result of chemical imbalances in the brain and, therefore, psychiatric drugs are the preferred treatment.

This theory appeals to pharmaceutical companies, insurance companies, psychiatrists, patients and often the relatives of the patients, though the appeal factor is different for each group. Pharmaceutical companies reap tremendous financial gain through sale of their drugs. Health insurance companies also reap financial gain by reducing the amount of money paid out for ongoing sessions of psychotherapy in addition to psychiatric drugs. The psychiatrist's role is simplified considerably when a biological factor of cause for mental disorders is emphasized over the psychosocial or environmental causes. Psychiatrists continue to be needed for their expertise in diagnosing mental disorders and in prescribing psychotropics, but they avoid the long-term, time-intensive sessions associated with psychotherapy. The patient and relatives are no longer responsible for changes that may need to be made in their own thinking, relationships or lifestyles and psychiatric drugs satisfy the desire for a quick-fix solution for the person's mental problems.

Biological Psychiatry

Most, though not all, psychiatrists believe the theory that ". . . every psychiatric disorder has an organic (that is, biological) component," and those that believe this theory are advocates for the use of psychotropics in treating mental disorders (Kaplan 336). The biological component translates into what psychiatrists hypothesize are chemical imbalances in the brain which cause mental disorders. Based on this theory, the treatment for the chemical imbalances is a chemical (a drug). **Nevertheless, there really is no definite proof that chemical imbalances are responsible for mental disorders**. "The public is told that a great deal of science is involved in the prescription of psychiatric drugs." However, Dr Breggin does not agree with this propaganda (5). He stated,

> Almost all psychiatric drug research is done on the normal brains of animals, usually rats. . . . [M]uch of this research involves grinding up brain tissues to investigate the gross effects of a drug on one or more limited biochemical reactions in the brain. More sophisticated research involves micro-instrumentation that injects small amounts of drugs into the living brain and measures the firing of brain cells. Yet even these more refined methods are gross compared to the actual molecular activity in the brain. . . . [We] have no techniques for measuring the actual levels of neurotransmitters in the synapses between cells. *Thus all the talk about biochemical imbalances is pure guesswork.* More important, what's actually being studied is the disruption of normal processes by the intrusion of foreign substances [drugs]. (7) (Italics mine)

According to Dr. Breggin, the research described above does not prove that psychiatric drugs correct imbalances, but rather proves that these drugs create imbalances. He further stated,

> In modern psychiatric treatment, we take the single most complicated known creation in the universe—the human brain—and pour drugs into it in the hope of "improving" its function when in reality we are disrupting its function. (7)

Many years prior to reading Dr. Breggin's book, *Your Drug May Be Your Problem*, I had already come to the conclusion that there is no definite proof of a chemical imbalance being the cause of mental disorders. While employed as the administrator of a home care agency, I had the opportunity to discuss at length the topic of chemical imbalances in relation to mental disorders with a Licensed Clinical Social Worker (LCSW). This man was the manager of the outpatient mental health center that was owned by the same corporation as the agency I managed. He explained to me that it is not really possible to know if mental disorders are caused by a chemical imbalance; however, there is believed to be a chemical imbalance based on the treatment protocol being a chemical [a drug]. Given this rationale a patient being prescribed a psychotropic should be informed that psychiatric medications (chemicals) are *known* to alter brain function, but what is *not known* is whether the end result of taking a psychotropic will be positive or negative. Informing the patient that he has a chemical imbalance that will be corrected by taking a psychotropic is simply not a true statement.

Dr. Breggin brings clarity to this debate by the following statement, "As confirmed in animal research, all psychiatric drugs directly affect the brain's normal chemistry by disrupting it" (34)

The Hypothetical Chemical Nature of Depression

Time does not permit us to examine all of the mental disorders and the speculations surrounding the biochemical dysfunction that may be the cause of each disorder. For that reason, we will confine our discussion to the proposed chemical imbalances that are thought to cause major depressive disorder. In addition, we will briefly discuss the theory underlying the correction of those imbalances with the use of antidepressant medication.

Since chemical neurotransmission is the process that is ". . . affected by most drugs used in psychiatry" it would seem necessary that psychiatrists would have a good understanding of both the chemical neurotransmission process and the action of the psychiatric drugs on that process (Kaplan 130). Unfortunately, this is not the case.

Chapter three of *Synopsis,* entitled "The Brain and Behavior," covered the subject matter of neuroanatomy, neurophysiology and neurochemistry as related to neuropsychiatry. Throughout this chapter there were statements reflecting the hypothetical nature of the information being presented. For example, in the section of the chapter devoted to chemical neurotransmission the following statement was made:

> Peptide neurotransmitters *may* have a longer
> duration of action than either biogenic amine
> neurotransmitters or amino acid

neurotransmitters. In that sense, peptide neurotransmitters *may serve a neuromodulatory role at some synapses.* (Kaplan 131) (Italics mine)

In the same chapter the authors of *Synopsis* revealed their theory of the role of serotonin in the psychopathology of depressive and manic disorders, and the possible effect that an antidepressant may have on the chemical imbalance:

> The principal association for serotonin with a psychopathological condition is with depression, as *suggested* in the biogenic amine *hypothesis* of mood disorders. That hypothesis is simply that depression is associated with too little serotonin and that mania is associated with too much serotonin. As explained above for norepinephrine, *that simplified view is undoubtedly not entirely accurate.* The *permissive hypothesis* postulates that low levels of serotonin permit abnormal levels of norepinephrine to cause depression or mania. (Kaplan 141) (Italics mine)

> . . . virtually all antidepressants are *believed* to have their effects by increasing the amount of serotonin or norepinephrine or both in the synaptic cleft. . . (Kaplan 130) (Italics mine)

The previous references demonstrate the lack of knowledge and the speculative nature of both the information concerning the process of chemical neurotransmission in relation to depression and the effect of antidepressant drugs on that process. This is further complicated by the "not entirely accurate" biogenic amine hypothesis which is the basis for prescribing antidepressants for the treatment of mood disorders.

Synopsis listed several drugs considered to be major antidepressants: "the tricyclic and tetracyclic drugs and the monoamine oxidase inhibitors (MAOIs) . . . [and] the "serotonin-specific reuptake inhibitors (SSRIs)," The same drugs are used to treat many other psychiatric disorders such as ". . . eating disorders, panic disorder, obsessive-compulsive disorder, and borderline personality disorders." The effect of these drugs on a chemical level is the inhibition of the reuptake of serotonin by presynaptic neurons causing the chemical to sit longer in the synaptic cleft (Kaplan 976). According to *Synopsis*, "What the relative roles of serotonin and norepinephrine are in the pathophysiology of depression is still unclear"(Kaplan 139). An antidepressant that is prescribed for a patient may or may not alleviate depression and may in fact cause adverse effects so severe as to become a threat to the individual's life. Whether in psychiatry or any other field of medicine, the effects of antidepressants are known to be both unpredictable and, therefore, unreliable. The controversy surrounding the predictability of antidepressants began in December, 1987 when Eli Lilly's Prozac hit the market.

Immediately following Prozac being introduced on the market, many other pharmaceutical companies rushed to produce a similar class of drugs, which were referred to in the media with labels such as, "Wonder Drugs" (Editors of *Psychology Today*, 42) or "The Personality Pill" (title of an article in *Time* magazine by Toufexis, 61). Though most of the articles seemed to portray antidepressants as an emotional panacea [cure-all], some articles identified dangers regarding the use of these drugs.

One such article that appeared in *People* magazine entitled "Miracle Worker," was written by S. Avery Brown who interviewed Peter Kramer, psychiatrist and author of the book, *Listening to Prozac*. Dr. Kramer indicated that the effects of the *popular drug,* Prozac, were difficult to predict. He was quoted in the article as saying, "I think there may be four or five ways that Prozac can make people more suicidal—by causing mental or physical agitation and so on. But these many causes add up to few cases" (153). In response to Dr. Kramer's comment about there being only a few cases of people who experienced the adverse effect of suicidal thinking, one must consider the impact of this statement if the person were a close friend or relative who subsequently committed suicide. Also, at that time, there were significantly fewer number of people taking Prozac as compared to the current number.

When questioned how Prozac works, Dr. Kramer explained,

> "Prozac slows the uptake of serotonin so that the chemical sits in the synapse—the space between the nerve cells—longer. That makes communication between nerve cells more efficient. Beyond that, I don't think anyone knows exactly how Prozac changes a patient" (Brown 153)

In spite of the lack of knowledge concerning the new psychotropics, the drugs continued to grow in popularity.

Since the early 1990s, drug companies and psychiatrists have promoted the use of these medications to such a degree that they are as commonplace as Tylenol. Advertisements not only present these drugs as the remedy for most, if not all, emotional discomfort, but also as a panacea for what an individual may consider undesirable personality traits. The magical aura surrounding the drugs provokes the idea that prescription drugs might offer a degree of the same mind/mood-alteration and effects that street drugs offer—under a legal platform.

In discussing the use of antidepressants with individuals who are taking them, it is not uncommon to hear them say that they are able to get any medication they want by just telling the physician that they are still depressed. I have noticed that individuals I have worked with use their prescription drugs similar to a street drug methodology. For example, one young lady I was working with became discouraged about a circumstance in her life. She responded to her emotional discomfort by taking not only the medications that were currently prescribed for her, but also several other medications that were not part of her current regimen. Rather than discard the previously prescribed medications, she kept them for when she felt overwhelmed. She was over medicated and later informed me that she had slept for the majority of the next two days. After this incident, she resumed her regular medication regimen; nevertheless, this was not an isolated incident involving the indiscriminate use of her medications. On previous occasions she had overdosed herself and was hospitalized. On one occasion she sustained some irreversible heart damage.

In summary, as a society dedicated to the principle that there should be a quick-fix remedy for all of life's problems, including emotional discomfort, we have opened Pandora's box, and have yet to experience the repercussions that may ensue related to the unprecedented use of psychotropics.

Chapter Eleven

Psychotropics

A single chapter devoted to the subject of psychotropics could by no means present all of the pros and cons of this type of therapy. Hopefully, the information provided will serve to motivate the reader to do further study and to pray for God's guidance concerning this subject.

". . . [P]harmacotherapy [drug therapy] for mental disorders is one of the most rapidly evolving areas in clinical medicine. . . " (Kaplan 865). Most psychiatrists advocate the use of psychotropics in treating mental disorders, but not all psychiatrists are proponents of psychiatric drug therapy. In fact, in September 1998, the International Center for the Study of Psychiatry and Psychology (ICSPP) held a conference that dealt with the subject of *"Counseling and Psychotherapy Without Psychiatric Drugs"* (Breggin 219). Most, if not all psychiatrists, would agree that their knowledge of the overall effects of psychotropic drugs on the brain is limited as evidenced by the following statement:

> Drug therapy and other organic treatments of mental disorders may be defined as *attempts* to modify or correct pathological behaviors,

thoughts, or moods by chemical or other physical means. The relations between, on the one hand, the physical state of the brain and, on the other hand, its functional manifestations (behaviors, thoughts, and moods) *are highly complex, imperfectly understood,* and at the *frontier of biological knowledge.* (Kaplan 865) (Italics mine)

Likewise, Dr. Breggin in his book, *Your Drug May Be Your Problem,* explained the complexity of molecular biology in relation to the chemical messengers involved in neurotransmission and thus in brain function.

The human brain has more individual cells (neurons) that there are stars in the sky. Billions! And each neuron may have 10,000 or more connections (synapses) to other brain cells, creating a network with trillions of interconnections.

Those trillions of interconnections between brain cells . . . are mediated by hundreds of chemical messengers (neurotransmitters). . . . We have limited knowledge about how a few of these chemical messengers work but little or no idea as to how they combine to produce brain function.

Nor do we have a clear idea about the relationship between brain function and mental phenomena such as "moods" or "emotions" like depression or anxiety. (5)

"Because of incomplete knowledge regarding the brain and the disorders that affect it, the drug treatment of mental disorders is empirical" (Kaplan 865). Empirical is defined as "capable of being verified or disproved by observation or experiment." Psychotropic therapy is empirical because psychiatric medications affect each individual in a different way. Multiple variables are known to influence the outcome of the treatment, necessitating ongoing observation to determine what *Synopsis* explained are the ". . .expected benefits, and the potential risks of pharmacotherapy." For that reason the patient, relatives, nursing staff, mental health workers and general practitioners all need to be knowledgeable about the adverse effects of psychiatric medications (Kaplan 865). Psychotropic therapy is also empirical because drug therapy may result in long-term adverse effects that will only be realized after the damage has already been done. In no other group are the risks of long-term adverse effects of psychotropics so ominous as they are in children.

Psychotropic Therapy for Children

To do justice to the subject of the use of psychotropics for children would necessitate writing another book. Nevertheless, a few references will serve to alert the reader to the dangers involved in medicating the minds of children and teens. Dr. Thomas Armstrong, a psychologist who has worked with children who have attention and behavioral problems, wrote a book entitled *The Myth of the A.D.D. Child: 50 Ways to Improve Your Child's Behavior and Attention Span Without Drugs, Labels, or Coercion.* Dr. Armstrong advocates the use of non-drug approaches in helping children to overcome their behavioral or attention problems. One of the main concerns he identified with the use of psychotropics for children is the possibility of long-term adverse effects. Dr. Armstrong made the following statement:

> . . .[T]he *Physicians' Desk Reference* section on Ritalin reports that "sufficient data on safety and efficacy of long-term use of Ritalin in children are not yet available." Since amphetamines create changes in brain chemistry, University of South Florida psychology professor Diane McGuinness **warns,** "The amphetamines interact with dopamine and norepinephrine. The consequences of a prolonged use of amphetamines could produce subsequent changes in the production and action of these two neurotransmitters." The consequences of this are unknown at present. However, one study appearing in the journal *Psychiatry Research* reported a significantly greater frequency of cerebral atrophy (abnormalities in the brain) in young adult males who had taken stimulant drugs like Ritalin during childhood, speculating that their drug treatments may have been a possible cause.

Concern regarding long-term adverse effects associated with psychotropic drug use in the treatment of children and teens was also reported in the November 3, 2003 issue of *TIME* magazine in an article written by Jeffrey Kluger entitled "Medicating Young Minds." Kluger discussed concerns of both the medical community and the families of children who are being medicated with psychotropics for either mood or behavioral problems. Kluger stated that ". . . concern is growing about just what psychotropic drugs can do to still developing brains" (51). Nevertheless, he also identified the nonchalant attitude that prevails in our American culture in spite of the possible long-term risks associated with psychotropic therapy.

> But few deny either that we're a *quick-fix culture*, and if you give us a feel-good answer to a complicated problem, we'll use it with little thought of long-term consequences. (51) (Italics mine)

Unfortunately, there is far less media coverage regarding the adverse effects of psychotropics on children than there is of the pro-drug media propaganda and advertisements by pharmaceutical companies promoting the drugs for children.

In a June 21, 2004 article in *The Wall Street Journal* entitled "Article About Antidepressant Stokes Debate on Transparency," there were some critical issues raised with regard to the known adverse effects of psychotropics prescribed for children, and the attempt by pharmaceutical companies to withhold findings of negative clinical drug studies. The following statement was made in that article:

> The APA [American Psychiatric Association], among others, has raised serious questions about some drug manufacturers' practice of actively seeking to publish positive clinical studies about their products

while giving negative ones little or no visibility. A number of unpublished studies of children taking antidepressants suggest the drugs aren't as effective as the published studies show. *The unpublished studies also suggest a greater risk of suicidal thinking than the published studies do.* (Windham & Martinez B5) (Italics mine)

The consequences of the public not being made aware of the life-threatening adverse effects of psychotropic drugs on children are greatly increased when considering the significant knowledge deficit surrounding psychotropic therapy in general. In Kluger's article, he quoted Dr. Glen Elliot, director of the Langley Porter Psychiatric Institute's children's center at the University of California, San Francisco, as having made the following statement regarding the use of psychotropics for children:

> "The problem is that our usage has outstripped our knowledge base. *Let's face it, we're experimenting on these kids without tracking the results.*" (51) (Italics mine)

Dr. Armstrong also expressed concern about the American quick-fix mentality in regard to children's mood and behavioral problems that has led to the popularity of choosing to deal with those problems with psychiatric drugs. Dr. Armstrong stated,

> For this brave new world of drugs has now made it possible for parents and professionals to encourage compliance in children through

purely biological means. All the messiness involved in growing up—the battle of the child's will against the adult's will, the endless restless curiosity, the sudden bursts of anger, excitement, or jealousy—all this unpleasantness can now be avoided. One simply needs to classify the unruly child in a soundly scientific framework, give him a diagnostic label—attention deficit disorder—and control him through a psychopharmaceutical cornucopia of state-of-the-art medications. (37)

The subtitle of Dr. Armstrong's book, *50 Ways to Improve Your Child's Behavior and Attention Span Without Drugs, Labels, or Coercion,* portrays his desire and efforts to help parents resolve their children's mood or behavioral problems without drug therapy. Nevertheless, as Christians it is even more important that we realize that God is both able and willing to heal, deliver and bless our children with a sound mind. As the scripture in Acts 2:39 reveals, the gift of the Holy Ghost is a promise ". . . unto you, and to your children, and to all that are afar off, even as many as the Lord our God shall call." For those reading this book who are not currently attending a church, I would highly recommend visiting a church where both you and your children could learn about and experience receiving the gift of the Holy Ghost. The Holy Spirit is the avenue by which God will bring about a transformation not only in your life, but also in your minds (Romans 12:2).

Psychotropics: Panacea or Assault?

In recent years, the National Institute of Mental Health (NIMH) has been collaborating with drug companies to promote psychiatric medications. By calling its campaigns "Anxiety Awareness Week" or Depression Awareness Week," it gives them a seemingly benign "educational" aura. Meanwhile, the drug companies themselves have helped to finance these activities. Some of these companies advertise directly to the public to convince people that they are depressed or anxious and thus "need" drugs. (Breggin 89)

Dr. Breggin's concern is that the success of these campaigns has resulted in Americans accepting and believing that emotional discomfort is a disorder. Both drug companies and physicians stand to benefit financially from the increased "awareness" of the symptoms of mental disorders such as clinical depression, panic disorder, or ADHD (90). The average person is so "aware" of the symptoms associated with mental disorders that often a self-diagnosis is made followed by a visit to the physician to receive what the drug company advertisement has portrayed as the quick-fix medication that will resolve the chemical imbalance in his brain. Family practitioners are prescribing more and more psychotropics following a short conversation with a patient who simply states he is depressed or anxious. This practice raises a red flag of concern even with psychiatrists who advocate the use of psychotropics. They are concerned that the family practitioners are not closely following the patient's reactions to the medications. The authors of *Synopsis* believe:

> The prescription of drugs for mental disorders must be made by a qualified practitioner and requires continuous clinical observation. Treatment response and the emergence of adverse effects must be monitored closely. The dosage of the drug should be adjusted accordingly, and appropriate treatments for emergent adverse effects must be instituted as quickly as possible. (Kaplan 865)

The seriousness of the emergence of adverse effects as mentioned above is supported by the results of an international survey that was done in 1998 that confirmed that psychiatric drug treatment,

> . . . frequently does more harm than good. More than 50 percent of patients drop out of psychiatric drug treatment "due to side effects," including drug-induced "sleep problems, anxiety, and agitation, and sexual dysfunction" (Breggin 31).

Given the preceding information, it is not surprising that Kaplan has reported: "Some patients may view a drug as a panacea, and other patients may view a drug as an assault" (865).

Dr. Breggin warned that anyone taking psychiatric drugs may experience one or more of the following common adverse effects:

- Impaired Concentration
- Poor Memory
- Confusion or Disorientation
- Slowed or Simplified Mental Functioning
- Exaggerated Responses to Stress
- Increased Irritability, Anger, or Aggressivity
- Sleep Difficulties
- Emotional Blunting and Insensitivity
- Fatigue
- Malaise (feeling ill, worn out, or blah)
- Depression
- Reduced Imagination and Creativity
- Impaired Self-Insight, Self-Understanding, or Self-Awareness
- Feeling "Out of Touch" with Yourself or Others
- Personality Changes
- Emotional Instability
- Anxiety
- Euphoria and Mania
- Neurological Problems, Including Spasms and Seizures
- Withdrawal and Rebound (52-56)

This extensive, but not all-inclusive, list of possible adverse effects represents probably only the tip of the iceberg of assaults that an individual could experience.

Dr. Breggin also pointed out that a physician's quick decision to prescribe a psychiatric drug may be the beginning of a lifetime of drug use:

> In today's prodrug environment, a doctor only takes a few minutes to make an evaluation before writing a prescription for an

antidepressant or tranquilizer. But your decision to accept medication may lead to a lifetime of drug use, including exposure to long-term harmful effects. Furthermore, whereas it was easy to find a doctor to start you on psychiatric drugs, it may be very hard to find one who is willing to help you stop. (16)

It is very disconcerting that most individuals given a prescription for a mind/mood-altering drug have not been diagnosed through a comprehensive mental and physical examination. And, they may or may not have a practitioner who is going to follow them closely for the development of adverse effects. For any individual who is on a psychiatric medication the following questions should be given consideration:

- Was it the individual's self-diagnosis that led to the physician's diagnosis? Was the self-diagnosis based primarily on the influence of advertisements from drug companies that continually bombard the public, advertisements that list the symptoms suggestive of a mental disorder and explain that these symptoms are the result of a chemical imbalance? (Very likely)
- Did the individual expect to receive a prescription for a psychotropic from the physician and did he get what he expected? (Usually)
- Does the medication live up to its "panacea" effect as was promoted by the advertisement? (Not usually)

- How did the physician determine the individual had a chemical imbalance?
- What laboratory tests were performed to validate the chemical imbalance?

As was discussed in chapter ten, a physician does not know if, in fact, there is a chemical imbalance. According to the authors of *Synopsis*, "No laboratory tests in psychiatry can confirm or rule out such diagnoses as schizophrenia, bipolar I disorder and major depressive disorder" (Kaplan 281). What degree of "scientific" or "medical expertise" is involved then in the decision to prescribe a psychotropic? Probably more often than not, both the diagnosis and the treatment are the result of a reaction by the patient to the pharmaceutical companies persuasive advertisement.

Unfortunately, most Americans and even most Christians have so much confidence in the pharmaceutical companies advertisements, and in the medical and psychiatric professions, that they usually do not inquire further as to what is meant by a chemical imbalance. Nor do they typically ask for details about the adverse effects of the medications that are prescribed. They have already been conditioned to believe that the drugs will resolve the chemical imbalance and will "fix" their emotional discomfort.

A few years ago, I attended a conference which dealt with the subject of biological psychiatry. The speaker spent a significant amount of time discussing the physiological aspects of stress-induced behavioral depression. He went on to discuss the current use of antidepressants and what is believed to be the chemical function of these medications within the brain.

During a break, I approached the speaker and asked several questions about the use of antidepressants. One of the first questions I asked was regarding my own observation of individuals who are on antidepressants, but continue to feel depressed. He explained that everyone responds differently to psychotropic medications. He further explained that a psychiatrist will often try several different types of antidepressants in an attempt to find which medication or combination of medications will be the most therapeutic for an individual. The goal is that a desired therapeutic response will be achieved which will provide a window of opportunity—a time when the individual's depressed state is improved. *Ideally,* during this window of opportunity, which may last from only a few hours to a few weeks, the therapist will *hopefully* maximize this opportunity by using psychotherapy to help the individual gain insight into his psychological problems. The speaker also stated that if the opportunity is missed, the individual might become more depressed.

With regard to the information given thus far about the use of psychotropics as a treatment modality for mental disorders, it has already been established that the cause of most mental disorders is not known. The treatment with psychotropics is advocated though there is a considerable lack of knowledge concerning exactly how these drugs will affect individuals. Individuals with mental disorders are told that they have a chemical imbalance. They are given this information based on the popularity of chemical treatment, not on the basis of a true laboratory test that has validated a chemical imbalance. As was stated in the preceding reference to depression, it is hoped that if a window of opportunity is achieved through the use of an antidepressant, it will last long enough for a therapist to do the following:

- Recognize the opportunity while it exists: which would be most unlikely, because, for many patients the practitioner who prescribed the medication will probably not see the patient again for a few weeks or months.
- Maximize the opportunity to use psychotherapy in hopes of assisting the individual to gain insight into his psychological problem
- Determine if the psychotherapy produced positive results and, if not, assess for signs of increased depression after the window of opportunity closes

With the heightened degree of uncertainty that exists in what appears to be this game of chance, why take the risk at all, if there is a more reliable and predictable remedy? With all the promises that are afforded by the Word and the Spirit of God, how could it be wiser for a Christian to put his trust in an inferior power, a power that may in fact be the subtle plan of the prince of this world? Hasn't Satan from the beginning of time offered to man a mere imitation of the real? Are psychiatric drugs a good substitute for the ". . . peace of God, which passeth all understanding," that ". . . shall keep your hearts and minds through Christ Jesus?" (Philippians 4:7).

A close friend of mine was advised by a psychiatrist to take an antidepressant. She had suffered many years in an abusive relationship, which ended when her husband was incarcerated. She was experiencing what I would prefer to call despair. Though she was faithful to church and loved God, her prayer life had waned. The exhaustion she felt from working a full-time job and raising three children as a single parent contributed to the feeling of overwhelming hopelessness. When I first met her, she told me she did not feel her relationship with God was what it needed to be, though it was evident that she loved the church and her Lord. She was experiencing several physical symptoms common to people who have emotional problems.

She made an appointment with her family practitioner, who, after *talking* with her, referred her to a physician who worked with patients on biofeedback for control of physical symptoms. The physician did not think she was a good candidate for biofeedback therapy and referred her to a psychiatrist. After a *short conversation* with the psychiatrist, he diagnosed her condition as depression and recommended that she start taking an antidepressant. He explained to her that due to the long-term stress she had been under, she was suffering from a chemical imbalance that could be corrected by taking the medication. [This explanation is not a factual or an accurate description of cause and effect. The physician did not know whether she had a chemical imbalance and, further, did not know if the antidepressant would correct the imbalance if one existed]. Since she did not like the idea of taking a mind/mood-altering substance, she agreed only to think about taking the medication.

Just prior to this series of medical appointments, she had started going to the church to pray in the mornings, and, though she continued to feel discouraged, I could see a noticeable improvement in her overall emotional state. Prayer is a very effective remedy for emotional problems. Since we had become close friends, she confided in me that she might start taking an antidepressant and wanted to know my thoughts regarding these medications. Being led by the Holy Ghost, I attempted to persuade her to continue to pray about this decision and reminded her that Jesus could heal and deliver her from the depression. I told her my testimony of how God had delivered me from depression. She made the decision not to start the medication and continued in her habit of morning prayer. A short time later during a series of revival services in the church, the Lord spoke to her and gave her a promise that He would intervene in the circumstances of her life. In a recent conversation she stated that she felt she had made the right decision and was anticipating the work that God would do in her life. She has continued with her early morning prayer practice; and now, five years later, has not had any further problem with depression. Also, within a relatively short period of time the Lord did work a miracle in the circumstances of her life.

Mind/Mood-Altering drugs

Dr. Breggin made the following comments with regard to the mind/mood-altering effects of psychotropics:

> You may sense that there is a cost to taking drugs—a dulling of your emotions, a slowing of your thinking processes or memory, a lackluster attitude toward life in general. (24)

In addition, psychotropics may alter an individual's ability to accurately assess the subtle or sometimes even acute changes in his own judgment, personality, character or moral integrity. We readily recognize the impaired judgment and personality changes of individuals using street drugs. Yet, we seem to be unaware that these same changes could be brought about by the use of prescription psychotropics.

As was mentioned in chapter ten, the authors of *Synopsis* believe that antidepressants increase the concentration of serotonin in the synaptic cleft, though they also explained that the role serotonin "in the pathophysiology of depression is still unclear" (Kaplan 139). In the same chapter of *Synopsis* the following information was given:

> Serotonin is also involved in the mechanism of at least two major substances of abuse [street drugs]. . . (LSD) and . . . (MDMA) also know as ecstacy. The serotonin system is the major site of action for LSD, but exactly how LSD exerts its effects remains *unclear*. (Kaplan 141) (Italics mine)

There does not appear to be any greater understanding of the action of antidepressants than there is of street drugs, yet, under a legal platform individuals who are already known to have emotional problems are given mind/mood-altering drugs to be taken usually without any direct supervision.

As Christians, we need to be cognizant of both the limitations of man and the omniscience of God. Do we really believe that God has all knowledge and that He can do all things? If we do, then our confidence and trust must be in Him. According to Psalm 118:8, "It is better to trust in the Lord than to put confidence in man." This becomes a critical factor when a Christian is considering the use of medications which alter the normal function of the brain and subsequently alter his thoughts, perceptions and emotions. Such mind/mood-altering effects may result in serious mental, physical and spiritual consequences. Dr. Breggin, in referencing information previously compiled by his coauthor Dr. David Cohen, made the following statement: "Scientific evidence can be marshaled to support the hypothesis that most psychiatric drugs "work" by producing a kind of anesthesia of the mind, spirit, or feelings." It is interesting that the subtitle of the section in chapter two where he made this statement was entitled "Anesthesia of the Soul" (36).

In working with patients in a nursing role, and with Christians in the role of a spiritual mentor, I have consistently observed that individuals taking psychotropics not only experience a "blunting" of their emotions, but also an impaired mental acuity. The following list depicts some of the spiritual problems that a Christian may experience while under the influence of a psychotropic medication.

- Decreased sensitivity to God (emotional blunting): First and foremost, I have noticed almost without exception that Christians who are on psychotropics express that they are not able to feel God. This is true whether they are in a church service or even when they pray alone at home. Though they may be faithful to church and find the sermons interesting, they do not "feel" anything and, therefore, often do not respond to the message or the altar call. Repentance, for example, is not only a realization of the need to change one's thoughts and behaviors, but repentance is frequently accompanied by a feeling of godly sorrow which gives rise to tears and a crying out to God for forgiveness and help to overcome. In addition, the fervent prayer of a righteous man that "availeth much" is a product of a man knowing he needs God to intervene, along with an intense desire or feeling that inspires his fervent prayer. In contrast, the inability to feel joy diminishes a Christian's strength. As was recorded in Nehemiah 8:10, ". . . for this day is holy unto our Lord: neither be ye sorry; for the joy of the Lord is your strength." And finally, loving God or our fellow man becomes a muted experience when void of emotion. A Christian whose emotions are blunted may attend church week after week, month after month and year after year, and neither respond to the messages nor be motivated to act on the changes that he may realize need to be made in his life.

- Decreased mental acuity: As Dr. Breggin points out, psychotropics may cause impaired concentration, poor memory, and slowed mental functioning (52). I have noticed when teaching Bible studies or even when discussing a subject with individuals who are on psychotropics that they have difficulty concentrating and focusing on the information being given. For this reason, I often limit the subject matter of the study and will use multiple examples to arrive at the same point or conclusion in order for them to comprehend and internalize the information.

- Diminished tolerance for circumstances that could cause stress, anxiety or insecurity: Often, Christians who are on psychotropics strive to control their environment and relationships to avoid what they consider to be an uncomfortable or vulnerable circumstance. More often than not, this problem leads to their isolating themselves from people or activities and may lead to their occasionally or even frequently missing church.

- Insomnia: Since many psychotropics have the adverse effect of causing insomnia, an individual may experience increased emotional instability related to sleep deprivation.

- Decreased self-control and/or moral integrity: Any individual taking mind/mood-altering drugs could experience the same adverse effects as individuals who take street drugs. People under the influence of legal and illegal drugs have been known to commit acts of violence or immorality that they probably would not have committed had they been drug-free. While working as a home care nurse, I remember a story that was told to me by the caregiver of one of my patients. Although some details must be withheld, the following is a brief summary of the account: One of the caregiver's relatives was taking care of her sister-in-law's five children in addition to her own three children. The woman and her husband believed it was their duty both as relatives and as Christians to provide a home for the abandoned children. As time passed, the responsibility of caring for the children became overwhelming and the woman felt trapped under the heavy burden. She went to a psychiatrist who diagnosed her condition as depression and subsequently prescribed an antidepressant for her. In spite of being medicated with an antidepressant, her depression became more severe and during a very emotionally unstable time, she reacted by using physical force in disciplining one of the children. Tragically, the child was injured and the injuries resulted in the death of the child. This type of behavior was totally out of character for this woman.

- Diminished or absent instinct of fear: Fear is a God-given instinct that warns and protects us when we are confronted with danger. Gavin De Becker, author of the book *The Gift of Fear*, has been called upon by the federal government to develop systems to prevent violence against high-ranking public officials and by numerous corporations and agencies to prevent violence in the workplace (Appendix Five). De Becker vividly depicts the instinctive nature of man's intuition of fear and self-preservation to not only alert an individual to imminent danger, but to provide knowledge of an immediate response that would avert the danger (25-28). Since psychotropics compromise mental acuity, an individual's ability to perceive the danger in a circumstance is hindered. For a Christian, an altered ability to correctly perceive life's circumstances, including those that involve danger, could lead to serious consequences. I have personally known of individuals who, while under the influence of psychotropics, felt absolutely no fear when confronted with obvious and in one case even life-threatening danger.

- Vulnerability to suicide: As was mentioned above, fear and self-preservation are God-given instincts that protect an individual. In addition, fear is also a learned response to teaching about circumstances and choices that could result in harmful or negative repercussions. For example, I was closely associated with a Christian woman who had been

149

taught that to take her own life would result in her being lost eternally for she believed God alone has the right to give and to take life. I was teaching her a series of Bible studies and over the course of time she confided in me that she was on several psychotropic medications. She explained that she had contemplated suicide many times before being on "psych meds," but had never tried to commit suicide because she had a fear of being lost. After being advised by a counselor to see a psychiatrist, she began taking the antidepressants that he had prescribed for her. She continued to suffer from severe depression in spite of those medications and some additional psychotropics that were added to her regimen in further attempts to treat her depression. None of the medications alleviated the depression she felt, and subsequently, she made a suicide attempt. Her testimony to me was that she believed she would never have attempted suicide had she not been on the medications. After starting the psychotropics, she no longer felt a fear of being lost if she committed suicide. In retrospect, I believe that had I been on antidepressants during the time I was struggling with thoughts of suicide, I would have attempted suicide. I remember a spiritual attack that came against me one day while driving home from work. The thought entered my mind that maybe I could fool God and just lose control of my car and kill myself. Immediately, however, I realized that God would know the truth and I would be lost. My fear of being lost, coupled with my love for my children and the belief that my children needed me, helped me to resist the devil and the temptation to commit suicide.

When in the history of mankind has it ever been more beneficial to put our confidence and trust in the wisdom of man rather than in God? Christians are instructed in the Word of God to ". . . be not conformed to this world: but be ye transformed by the renewing of your mind, that you may prove what is that good, and acceptable, and perfect, will of God" (Romans 12:2). The Word of God also asks us to consider, "Are ye so foolish? having begun in the Spirit, are ye now made perfect by the flesh?" (Galatians 3:3). "For God has not given us the spirit of fear; but of power, and of love, and of a sound mind" (II Timothy 1:7). God will make Himself very real to anyone who commits his life to Him and He will reward those that diligently seek Him (Hebrews 11:6).

In ministering to individuals who are on psychotropics, it is imperative to let the **Lord be their guide** with regard to the discontinuation of the medications they are taking. **Christian mentors are not responsible to recommend that an individual stop taking his medications, as God knows the perfect timing for this action.** The individuals I have worked with have not experienced any problem discontinuing their medications when they were led by God to do so. In chapter sixteen, there will be testimonies of people who have been led by the Lord to stop taking their psychotropics and the result of their actions.

In summary, I believe that man is so inferior to God that he could not possibly discover or comprehend all there is to know about the brain and its functions. Secondly, to completely understand the brain and the functions of the mind, man would of necessity need to understand all the operations of the spirit world since the Spirit of God and the spirits in this world influence man's thoughts. Thirdly, psychology, unlike other sciences, finds itself continually in a checkmate dilemma, "Ever learning and never able to come to the knowledge of the truth" (II Timothy 3:7).

God has blessed man's endeavors in every other science, allowing man to discover and perform unimaginable feats of both a scientific and medical nature. Consider, for example, the transplanting of a human heart. But, God has created the brain, the seat of man's mind and emotions, with such complexity as to be out of the reach of man's complete comprehension. Why? Because the mind is the doorway to the soul. **With the mind, we choose to repent and deny our own self-rule, and with the mind we choose to serve God.**

Part Two

More Than Conquerors

. . . [W]e are more than conquerors through him that loved us. For I am persuaded, that neither death, nor life, nor angels, nor principalities, nor powers, nor things present, nor things to come, Nor height, nor depth, nor any other creature, shall be able to separate us from the love of God, which is in Christ Jesus our Lord. (Roman 8:37-39)

. . . [The] anointing which ye have received of him abideth in you . . . the same anointing teacheth you of all things, and is truth, and is no lie, and even as it hath taught you, ye shall abide in him. (I John 2:27) [The anointing is in reference to the gift of the Holy Spirit].

Chapter Twelve

Humpty Dumpty

The remaining chapters are devoted to a discussion of some of the principles that God has taught me, which have enabled me to maintain a sound mind and to be victorious in living for Him. I John 2:14 teaches Christians that because the Word of God abides in them, they can "overcome the wicked one." Also, as children of God, we are victorious because, ". . . greater is he that is you [us] than he that is in the world" (I John 4:4). Nothing can separate us from the love of God and "We love him, because he first loved us" (I John 4:19). Satan, however, continually attempts to deceive Christians about God's love and concern for them. Individuals who are emotionally unstable are particularly vulnerable to this deception.

Emotionally crippled people often fall prey to the deception that God neither cares about their circumstances and suffering nor does He understand what they are going through. Another misconception that these individuals are prone to is that God judges them and their circumstances the same way humanity judges. Unlike people—who judge from a perspective of what they see and hear—God knows the truth about all of our circumstances and He knows our hearts. He is a righteous judge who responds to the needs of humanity with mercy and compassion. According to Isaiah 11:1-4:

> And there shall come forth a rod out of the stem of Jesse, and a Branch shall grow out of his roots: And the spirit of the Lord shall rest upon him, the spirit of wisdom and understanding, the spirit of counsel and might, the spirit of knowledge and of the fear of the Lord; And shall make him of quick understanding in the fear of the Lord: and *he shall not judge after the sight of his eyes, neither reprove after the hearing of his ears*: But with righteousness shall he judge the poor, and reprove with equity for the meek of the earth. . . . (Italics are mine)

Emotionally unstable individuals often bear the reproach of the circumstances that contributed to their crippled emotional state. For example, it is not uncommon for emotionally crippled people, particularly those who have suffered abuse from someone close to them, to think that they are to blame for their circumstances and their relationship conflicts. Those in abusive relationships believe this deception for three reasons. First, the individual administering the abuse has told them that they are to blame for how they are being treated. Secondly, if they refuse to accept the blame and do not offer an apology or behave in a manner that demonstrates contrition, the abuse will usually increase in frequency and severity. Thirdly, the deception of misplaced blame is often reinforced by those around them who judge both people and circumstances only by what they see and hear. Thus, emotionally crippled people often suffer under a load of overwhelming hopelessness and guilt:

- Guilt for not being able to snap out of the mental state they are in, as most people suggest is possible
- Guilt for all the things they are not doing and guilt for the things they are doing, that bring little or no satisfaction
- Guilt for those they seem to hurt and for the burden they are to everyone
- Guilt about relationships with others, believing they are to blame for their relationship conflicts
- Hopelessness based on their past experiences of trying desperately and in vain to change the circumstances of their lives and the conflicts in their relationships
- Hopelessness due to unending stress and discouragement with no apparent relief in sight
- Hopelessness because strength is gone and the joy of life is but a fleeting illusion
- Hopelessness because life has lost its meaning and death seems more appealing than life

During the six-year emotional valley that I had traveled through, I remember my own attempts to convince those around me that I had not always been emotionally crippled, hoping that they would not view me in such a negative light. The seemingly futile attempts to receive compassion from humanity led me to yield to the deception that God did not care or have compassion toward me. This misconception led to another deception—that God was punishing me and, therefore, I deserved what I was going through. Nevertheless, God was able to break the yoke of oppression and to help me understand that He does not judge by what *appears* to be the circumstances surrounding our lives. Likewise, He assured me that my circumstances and my emotionally crippled state were not the result of His punishment.

Judging the heart of God by what we observe in humanity is a tragic mistake! God, indeed, had great compassion on me; and He chose to make me aware of His compassion in a most explicit manner. The following incident took place a few months prior to my deliverance from the spiritually oppressed state I was in, which was previously described in chapter five. The circumstances of my life had left me feeling like only a shell of a human being. In the midst of what seemed to be a whirlwind of life crises, the shell of my life was smashed and broken into a million pieces. During this desperate and hopeless time, I decided to record in a diary what I was experiencing, however, being unable to be disciplined in this effort, I recorded my thoughts and feelings for only a few days. The following excerpts depict the extremity of the hopelessness I was experiencing:

4:45 A.M.

Fear, depression, hopelessness, and despair. . . Only God can help me now! No human being can protect me, heal me, and put me back together again. Prayed, but no faith; can't hear God because I can't believe. Called work, will not be able to go in. Anxiety ridden, can barely think, my thoughts are a confused mess.

9:00 A.M. [the same day]

My 14-year-old son gives me a hug and I sense his love, but he cannot help me. My 8-year-old daughter senses my depression and great concern covers her face, *"Mom, what's wrong?"* Drew is tired but cooperative [Drew was 4 at this time]. My children are so kind to me. I know I love them, but years of depression have taken their toll and it's difficult to give what I do not have. Will this ever end? Will I ever be healed? Why?

My mental state was deteriorating and only through great effort and determination was I able to continue to work a job. One day while at work, I was overcome with feelings of tremendous despair and loneliness. Approximately one year had passed since my husband had moved out of our home. In my desperate state of mind that day, I questioned the Lord as to whether He knew or even cared about what I was going through. [Satan so cunningly portrays the deception that God is oblivious to our emotional pain]. While pondering these thoughts, I glanced at my desk calendar and noticed that I had scheduled an interview with a prospective employee and anticipated that she would be arriving in just a few minutes. I struggled to pull myself out of my distracted and tormented state of mind to conduct the interview. When the woman entered my office, I was immediately drawn to her, sensing somehow a bond, though this was our first meeting.

During the course of the interview, she mentioned that her desire for employment was not based on a financial need, but rather to help occupy her time. She stated that since her husband's death, two years ago, she had been very lonely and had begun to realize she needed a change in her life. She thought that being employed might alleviate some of the loneliness she was experiencing. Though I usually avoided discussing personal matters during interviews, I could not resist the urge I felt to ask about her relationship with her husband.

"Did you have a good relationship with your husband?"

She smiled as she began to reflect. She spoke freely and affectionately of their relationship and began a narrative of what must have been some of her most cherished memories of her husband. From her recounting of past experiences and events, I realized that they had enjoyed a continuing romance throughout their marriage and that they had truly become as "one" in their relationship.

One of the memories she related was her initial meeting with her soon to be high school sweetheart and, thereafter, future husband. She was standing in the shallow water of the lake just in front of her parents' lake home when he walked up to her and began a conversation. Later, after they were married, the same lake home became their permanent residence and the place where they had shared many years of happiness. Apparently her reminiscing brought to her mind the tragic event that had taken her husband's life. Her countenance changed as sadness etched over her expression and as the memory of those events played out in her mind.

Without me requesting any details, she described the events that took place on that fateful day. Her husband had gone down to the lower walk-out level of their lake home to feed the dog and she remained in the level just above him. Suddenly, she heard the sounds of a deafening explosion that later was determined to be the result of a gas leak. Agonizing screams pierced the air from the lower level of their home. After running out onto the deck she realized she needed to reenter the house to call for help, but the door through which she had just exited was engulfed with flames. Hearing her husband's screams, and realizing the screams were now coming from outside the house just below where she was standing on the deck, she turned from the door and saw him running toward the lake. His clothes and body were on fire—he was burning like a human torch. Terror gripped her heart as she ran down the steps to join him in the lake where he was standing. There they stood close together, in the same place they had stood many years before when they had met for the first time.

There followed a period of silence during which neither she nor I could speak.

When she continued, she spoke of the consuming loneliness she had been experiencing for the last two years. I wanted desperately to comfort her. I knew shallow words of comfort would not suffice, so I confided in her and told her some of the details of my marriage that had ended with my husband leaving our home. We agreed that the loneliness was unrelenting and at times completely unbearable.

Her next comment shocked me, and only after that comment did I realize that Jesus had prearranged our meeting and was speaking through this woman to assure me that He both knew and cared about what I was going through. Her face and voice expressed tenderness and compassion as she spoke these words:

"You have suffered much more than I have."

I was so taken aback by this statement that I didn't know how to respond. Her story was one of the most tragic

I had ever heard, and I was amazed that she could think that my suffering was greater than her suffering. I solemnly returned her statement with a question.

"Why do you say that?"

She replied slowly and softly,

"Well,. . . I have suffered loss, but you have suffered both loss and rejection."

Immediately upon hearing those words I felt the presence of the Lord surround me, and with His presence came comfort and a new dimension of revelation about His love, compassion and profound knowledge. By allowing me to experience such a depth of compassion for this woman's suffering, He had revealed to me the depth of His compassion for me. I realized that He understood my circumstances and the degree of loneliness I continued to endure. The deception that Satan had so cunningly woven in my mind—that God did not care about what I was going through—was exposed and a door of healing and restoration was opened for me.

Divine Compassion

Dear Reader. . . there are nuggets of truth to be gleaned from this chapter. No matter how misunderstood you and your circumstances may seem to be by those around you, they are not misunderstood by God. Be very careful not to attribute to God the attitudes and actions that you may have experienced at the hands of men. He is omniscient and knows you, your life and your circumstances far better than you even know them yourself. Jesus loves you more than you could ever imagine. However, Satan would have you believe that God does not care about or understand your suffering and that your suffering is a result of God's punishment. The truth is that God is a most gracious, loving and compassionate Savior.

Deliverance from the oppression of Satan and the emotionally crippled state you are in, depends upon your believing that God loves you and that He desperately wants to help you. He has made provision for your emotional healing by His own suffering, and through His power your broken life and your fragmented state of mind can be put back together again. In fact, more likely than not, you will like the new person you will become even more than the old person you used to be.

When I was a child, the story of Humpty Dumpty always made me feel sad. Unlike many of the children's fairy tales, stories or poems, the ending was not a happy ending. The following is a revised rendition of the same poem, portraying that what is impossible with men is possible with God.

Humpty Dumpty sat on a wall,
Humpty Dumpty had a great fall;
All the King's horses, and all the King's men
Cannot put Humpty Dumpty together again.

But the King can!

Chapter Thirteen

Continued Deliverance

My testimony of the miraculous deliverance I experienced from the oppressive spirit of depression was given in chapter five. After being delivered from that spiritual oppression, the voices of my constant companions—hopelessness and despair—were silenced. Yet, there remained several other "strongholds" in my mind that also needed to be demolished. This chapter is a continuation of my testimony of how God guided me by His counsel, delivered me by His power and continued to transform me by the "renewing of my mind."

God is the author and finisher of our faith, and as we advance through His transformation process, He will change and mold us with the intent that we will be like Him. According to Romans 12:1-2, the transformation process takes place in our minds as we yield ourselves to His will:

> I beseech you therefore, brethren, by the mercies of God, that ye present your bodies a living sacrifice, holy, acceptable unto God, which is your reasonable service. And be not conformed to this world: but be ye

transformed by the renewing of your mind, that ye may prove what is that good, and acceptable, and perfect, will of God.

God provides counsel through the Scriptures and by His Spirit "in us," bringing about changes in the way we perceive, think and react to people and life's circumstances. Ultimately, Christ desires to be formed in us and to manifest Himself in our lives (Galatians 4:19). He must increase, and we, referring to our carnal nature, must decrease. We are unable to do this without a tearing down of the strongholds in our minds.

After an individual has received Christ's Spirit, he has both a carnal and a spiritual mind. Learning to walk in the Spirit is a process of learning to discipline our minds to think spiritually, as the carnal mind is not subject to the law of God (Romans 8:4-10). To be spiritually minded is to bring into captivity every thought to the obedience of Christ, enabling a Christian to have the mind of Christ. This truth has been referred to repeatedly throughout this book because it is a precept that must be deep-seated in the heart and mind of all Christians if they want to be like Christ.

Individuals who are emotionally crippled are often preoccupied with self-destructive thoughts patterns. In addition, they usually have a poor self-esteem and may even experience a loss of self-identity. Though I had been miraculously delivered from the oppression of Satan, I continued to struggle with self-destructive thought patterns that had taken root in my mind. My self-esteem was very poor and I had lost touch with my own spirit causing me to literally feel like I did not know myself. God's work of deliverance was not yet complete. Jesus would, in the near future, perform several miracles to transform or change me by renewing my mind as He continued to restore me to wholeness.

Miracles Unlimited

People who are emotionally unstable usually lack self-confidence and subsequently relate to other people and life through viewpoints which often are not their own—viewpoints that may have been imposed upon them through spiritual oppression or an abusive relationship. Over time, the quenching of their own spirit results in a loss of their self-identity.

Reflecting on the experience of having suffered a loss of self-identity, I remember that I yearned to know myself, to connect with my spirit that had long since been repressed. Many times I would look at my favorite childhood photograph of the little girl I used to be and wonder who I was now. It was no longer possible to relate to the child in the picture, but instinctively I knew that I would like that person better than the person I had become.

During that time in my life, I was employed as a nurse on the night shift in a private home caring for a medically fragile child. Since the child slept most of the night, there was a great deal of time to meditate and pray. One night, as I pondered again what it would be like to know myself, I whispered a prayer to God asking Him to please let me know myself. As the shift wore on, I really was not aware that anything had happened in response to my simple prayer; however, the next morning when leaving work I was keenly aware of a change in myself. Suddenly, I realized that I had regained a consciousness of my own spirit. Miraculously, I had been reunited with that young girl in the picture and even with some aspects of her personality. She had an inner zeal and enthusiasm for life and that morning I realized that a renewed enthusiasm for life had been restored to me. Regaining my self-identity was a vital part of the restoration process the Lord was performing in my life. To have meaningful relationships with other people, or even with God, a person must be in touch with his own spirit.

Another self-destructive pattern of thinking that persisted in my mind was that for many years the mirror had reflected only an image of human despair and the unmistakable countenance of hopelessness. My wardrobe reflected the state of my mind as most of my clothes were dark-colored and unattractive, plain styles. Though hopelessness and despair were no longer visible in my countenance, my thought patterns about my appearance remained unchanged. The stronghold of perceiving myself as ugly continued until God exposed this deception to me. Turning to God again in prayer, I asked Him to help me with my thoughts and feelings about my appearance. Over the next few weeks, many people gave me compliments about my appearance. Initially, my reaction to these compliments was to conclude that the people were just being friendly or kind. It did not occur to me that perhaps I was attractive. Nevertheless, the compliments brought about a change in the way I viewed myself. Shortly thereafter, I began to buy colorful, attractive clothing.

Another miracle that God performed came in response to a new emotional challenge that had emerged after I was delivered from the oppressive spirit of depression. My emotions vacillated between the extremes of happiness and sadness. Occasionally, and for no apparent reason, I also experienced frustration and anger. It occurred to me that during the six-year period that I was spiritually oppressed, my emotional state was consistently on the same plane—feeling only despair and hopelessness. With the return of other emotions, I had difficulty controlling the renewed emotions. The song, *Down in the Valley, Up on the Mountain,* could have been the theme song for my fluctuating emotional state. The mood swings, which were like riding a emotional roller coaster, became unbearable. Feeling desperate, I called a friend of mine and told her about the problem I was having and asked her, *"Will I ever be normal?"*

Her response to my question served only to escalate the desperation I was feeling. She explained, *"When a person has a single or short-term traumatic experience such as a woman being a victim of rape, she can usually be completely delivered from the emotional aftermath. But, if a person has suffered years of traumatic experiences, it is unlikely that she will ever be completely delivered or normal."*

After hearing her explanation, I felt devastated and tears streamed down my face. How could this be? Not only had I endured the difficult circumstances, but now I would never have a completely normal personality again. I cried out to God in prayer and then, as the psalmist David had done many times, I claimed for myself a promise of God. I said, *"God, it may be impossible that I will ever be normal or completely delivered, but you said you are the God of the impossible, and I want to be delivered from this now!"* A spirit of intercession came over me as I cried and prayed, and I began to speak in tongues. The Spirit of God made intercession through me as I prayed. After several minutes, quite abruptly, the language I was speaking changed to English allowing me to understand what the Spirit was praying through me. Much to my amazement, I was praying blessings upon an individual who had caused a great deal of pain and sorrow in my life. Thereafter, I do not remember experiencing mood swings again. Another part of my restoration had taken place. I realized, as never before, that God was willing to deliver me from *all* of my afflictions if I would just simply ask Him.

> Ask, and it shall be given you; seek, and ye shall find; knock, and it shall be opened unto you: For every one that asketh receiveth; and he that seeketh findeth; and to him that knocketh it shall be opened. (Matthew 7:7-8)

Digressing briefly, I would like to give a scriptural explanation of the above experience regarding the gift of tongues and interpretation. The apostle Paul wrote to the church at Corinth and gave the following instruction regarding the gift of tongues and interpretation:

> Wherefore let him that speaketh in an unknown tongue pray that he may interpret. For if I pray in an unknown tongue, my spirit prayeth, but my understanding is unfruitful. (I Corinthians 14:13-14)

There is also a scripture that explains that the Spirit of God will make intercession for us because there are times when we do not know what we should pray concerning our circumstances (Romans 8:26). My experience in prayer that day was both an example of the Spirit of God interceding for me and through me, as well as a manifestation of the gift of tongues and interpretation.

The blessings and miracles related thus far in this chapter had happened over only a few months. And, though I was both mentally and emotionally stable by this time, there was one final stronghold that continued to be a struggle for me. Strange as it may seem, I did not truly like or love myself. After years of entertaining negative thoughts about myself, it was difficult to love myself. Seeking God for help in this area took precedence in my prayers.

Interestingly, the change in my thought patterns concerning loving myself did not happen as quickly as the other miracles. In fact, months passed before I began to realize that I liked myself and considerably more time before I was able to love myself. The extended time for this prayer to be answered may have been related to the process of change that I was going through. God was helping me to see myself through His eyes and to engraft His thoughts into my perceptions about myself. Also, I realize that loving someone, whether yourself, another person or even God, is a learning process.

Part of loving myself was realizing and accepting that I did not have to be the perfect mother, Christian, employee, or friend. I was learning to be comfortable with just being me. As time passed, I could receive criticism from another person about myself and then stand back and evaluate if the criticism was valid and react appropriately. This is not to imply that it does not bother me to have people point out my shortcomings; rather, that I am able to deal with the comments more constructively because I love myself, and I am able to give myself the benefit of the doubt. Acknowledging that I have negative thoughts, character traits or behaviors is acceptable to me because I know that God will transform me if I will ask Him to do so.

Most emotionally crippled people, especially those who were abused, find it difficult to receive critiquing of any kind because they have such a poor self-esteem. They tend to believe others' evaluations of themselves instead of their own, resulting in the ever-futile reaction of trying to measure up to other people's expectations. Thus, they never please anybody. One person's criteria for positive character traits may be considered negative character traits by another individual. Therefore, as Christians we must strive to become like Jesus and allow His character to be formed in us.

Over time I realized that I had been transformed by the renewing of my mind, and had been restored to wholeness, but in a sense I was a new person. And, though I like the new person better than my "old self," I believe that the transformation process is an unending process of learning to think and act more like Jesus. One may ask how a person knows when he is emotionally healed or restored to wholeness. A good indicator of having been emotionally healed and restored to wholeness is when a person loves God, himself and others.

Chapter Fourteen

I Am a Worm and No Man

. . .Thou art holy, O thou that inhabitest the
praises of Israel. Our fathers trusted in thee:
they trusted, and thou didst deliver them.
They cried unto thee, and were delivered:
they trusted in thee, and were not confounded.
But I am a worm, and no man; a reproach of
men, and despised of the people.
(Psalm 22:3-6)

Psalm 22:6 is a passage of scripture that over the years
I had read many times and, yet, the meaning of the phrase
"I am a worm and no man" continued to be perplexing to
me. There seemed to be a revelation or depth of
understanding that I had not been able to comprehend. The
word "worm" does not seem an appropriate term to use in
reference to man and certainly not in a prophetic reference
to Jesus. The insight required to understand this scripture
came through a "valley experience" during which time I
occupied a "solitary place" with respect to close
relationships. The significance of this time in my life would
only be realized while writing this chapter.

Being an extrovert for most of my life allowed me to initiate conversations and friendships with relatively little effort. I remember a conversation I had with a friend as we traveled together to a church conference. While discussing the direction the Lord seemed to leading us in our lives, I began to relate to her the recurring thought that I believed the Lord was impressing on my mind. The words "solitary place" had come into my mind several times over the previous weeks, causing me to ponder these words and what they might mean in my life. Therefore, I anticipated that in the near future I would be going through a time when I would perhaps be deprived of the support and fellowship of close friends. Prior experiences had taught me not to attempt to avoid or resist a trial, as resisting only increased the suffering involved in the experience. We arrived at the conference and were both amazed when the preacher gave the title for his first sermon—*The Solitary Place*. Shortly thereafter, I entered the valley of the solitary place ultimately to learn about what a person experiences when he feels like a worm.

Several years later, when I was nearing the end of this trial, I felt the solitary place was totally unbearable. I began to pray fervently for the Lord to deliver me from the solitary place. Contemplating the years of loneliness, I hoped that the Lord had accomplished in my mind and heart the lesson He wanted me to learn.

Then one day while praying, I asked God again to deliver me out of the lengthy and difficult trial, and while talking to Him I heard myself exclaim, *"Lord, I'm just a worm!"* When the words came out of my mouth, I remembered the scripture in Psalms. I did not know why I had spoken those particular words; however, they were a perfect description of how I felt about myself at that moment. Over the next two days as I wrote this chapter, the Lord revealed to me the circumstances under which a human being could feel like a worm. Living in the valley—the solitary place—had now made the phrase, "I am a worm and no man," applicable to me.

A worm is not something that is feared; a worm is something that is avoided simply because of its somewhat repulsive appearance. If there is a worm on the sidewalk, I usually walk around it. Worms are not desirable in any way, so they are avoided. Emotionally crippled people frequently receive treatment from others that makes them feel like a worm. However, the reaction of others to them is often a result of their own negative behaviors.

We have all experienced talking to and attempting to help someone who is emotionally unstable and oppressed. The aura around these individuals is both oppressive and negative. The conversations are uncomfortable, often causing all participants to feel discouraged and hopeless. Spending a great deal of time with these individuals will drain a person emotionally and to no avail, since they usually continue in the same crippled state despite a considerable amount of effort spent in sympathizing, encouraging and consoling.

After a few encounters of this nature, people learn to avoid contact with emotionally crippled individuals whose countenances readily betray their emotional state. People develop a pattern of behavior toward them that is similar to one's reaction to a worm. Even Christians, when we see an emotionally crippled person walking toward us in church, will frequently engage ourselves in a conversation with another person or change our direction to avoid the person entirely. We console ourselves believing that the avoidance behavior went unnoticed, but not only did the hurting individual know he was being avoided, but he felt the sting of rejection once more. When internalized, the fresh wound of rejection causes even greater crippling. The emotionally unstable person, if not already convinced, is now assured that he is "a worm, and no man; a reproach of men, and despised of the people" (Psalm 22:6).

Feeling like a worm causes a person to think he owes an apology to humanity for the fault of his existence. Often, the individual will express this sentiment by saying something like: *"I wish I had never been born, but I had no say in the matter."* Satan capitalizes on these thoughts and expressions of despair by imposing on his mind the following suggestion: *You may not have had a say in whether you were born, but you do have a say in whether you have to keep on living.* As interpersonal relationships deteriorate, these individuals begin to consider life as not worth living. Understanding the perceptions of emotionally crippled individuals will enable the church to be compassionate when ministering to them. Frequently, the trials the Lord allows Christians to experience are meant to foster the character trait of compassion in them.

Sympathy or Compassion?

Trials are beneficial to the individual who is being tried, for if he endures the suffering, he will come forth as gold. Trials in the life of a Christian will also benefit other people who will receive comfort and encouragement from him. Through "valley experiences" or through trials in the "fiery furnace," a child of God will gain compassion for people who are suffering. God's desire is for His children to be like Him, and compassion is inherent in God's nature.

When someone is experiencing such a depth of despair that they feel they are not able to bear it any longer, they need to receive compassion, not sympathy. At best, sympathy only masquerades as compassion, and to the one in need, expressions of sympathy seem philosophical and distant.

Sympathy is defined as having common or shared feelings with another individual or group of individuals. Life's experiences enable us to sympathize with other people going through similar circumstances. Sympathy is a sufficient response if the individual you are ministering to is dealing with a rather minor circumstance or problem that needs no intervention. However, offering sympathy in response to the desperate needs of an emotionally crippled person is perhaps worse than no help at all. Compassion is what is required. Compassion in a Christian is born out of the "fiery trials" that remove the dross of our selfish nature and give liberty to the sacrificial nature of God's Spirit in us.

God has designed trials that will take His children through the "fiery furnace," which often must be endured for a long period of time. During these trials, an individual may think he is not able to bear the suffering another second. Yet, enduring the suffering changes one's sympathetic views to a heartfelt compassion. God's purpose in perfecting the attribute of compassion in our lives will be accomplished through these trials.

Compassion is defined as a "sympathetic consciousness of others' distress **together with a desire to alleviate it."** Compassion is a force that goes beyond just relating to what another individual is experiencing—it compels a Christian to do something to alleviate the person's suffering by whatever means possible. Search the

Scriptures and you will find that whenever it was said, "Jesus had compassion;" that statement was followed by a miracle or some action to alleviate the distress of the person on whom He had compassion. The single greatest act of compassion was portrayed when God became the sacrifice for our sins that we might know and understand the ultimate depth of His love and compassion.

Compassion drives an individual to "get involved," rather than just express sympathy. Compassion overlooks the injustices and hurts often reciprocated by those one is trying to help. Compassion embodies longsuffering, not allowing us to give up on individuals, but to minister to them in faith. Faith is the essence of seeing not what the individual is at the present, but what we believe he will be when God has done a work in his life. Emotionally crippled people need to know that God loves them and has compassion on them. They need to see this demonstrated through His body, the church. The deception that God does not love them or that He is punishing them must be overturned by the knowledge of the truth in His Word.

I remember that during my trial in the "solitary place" I questioned God as to whether I had done something to deserve what I was going through. He assured me that I was not being punished or even chastised, but that suffering was the tool by which He would develop compassion in me. As recorded in Isaiah 54:16, "Behold, I have created the smith that bloweth the coals in the fire, and that bringeth forth an instrument for his work. . . ."

Emotionally crippled people have difficulty believing that God will work on their behalf. They are vulnerable to the spiritual oppression of Satan who deceives them about God's love, forgiveness, healing, deliverance and salvation.

This type of spiritual oppression dictates the need to be ministered to by someone who,

- Has compassion and will pray, fast and intercede on behalf of hurting individuals for their deliverance from spiritual oppression
- Will teach them the Word of God, speaking faith to them
- Will overlook the appearance of the hopelessness of their life and teach them to believe that the God of glory is able to change anyone's life if submitted to Him in faith

For the emotionally crippled person, trusting is very difficult. They often think that submitting to any authority, even to the authority of the Lord, makes them vulnerable. Faith in people or God seems unattainable due to their previous experiences and rejections. Only love and compassion can bridge the gap for these individuals. As the church of Christ, Jesus desires His children to be His mouth, hands and feet and to minister to those that are hurting emotionally. Love and compassion are the only means by which the church can fulfill this ministry.

Chapter Fifteen

Mind-sets for Victory

Reflecting on the last 30 years of living for God, my testimony is that Jesus has never failed me. He has been my father, friend, protector, deliverer, healer, provider and anything that I needed Him to be. Life's experiences, since becoming a Christian, have left an indelible imprint on my mind of scriptural truths that govern my thoughts about life, myself, other people and God. They are treasures, "nuggets of truth," that are fixed in my mind and have become my *Mind-Sets For Victory*. Each subtitle in this chapter will introduce a scriptural truth, a sure foundation, which, when adopted as a mind-set, will stay your course in facing the storms of life. The list of mind-sets is inexhaustible since the Word of God is the source of these truths. These truths will be discussed in conjunction with the testimonies of other people with whom I have been or am at present closely associated. The individuals will not be identified by their own names with the exception of my brother Bob. I believe the greatest representation of Christ's love can be envisioned through the testimony of His children who have been comforted, healed, and delivered—set free from the bondage of sin and the oppression of Satan.

God Loves You and is For You

Most emotionally crippled people find it difficult to believe that they are loved and that someone has their best interest in mind. After sometimes years of abuse and rejection, they develop a pattern of thinking and behavior that resembles a survival mode of existence. Their defensive and non-trusting behaviors, which are believed to shield them from hurt, in reality only prevent them from experiencing close and meaningful relationships. Interpersonal encounters usually evoke the following questions in their mind: Is this person for me or against me? Will this encounter bring harm to me? Usually, even if the other individual is relating in a very positive manner, the encounter may still be perceived as negative due to their distrustful and skeptical type of thinking.

Unfortunately, the defensive behaviors of the emotionally unstable person permeate every part of his life, hindering not only his relationships with other people, but also his relationship with God. Negative life experiences elicit the perspective that God is against him or that He is punishing him. Satan fuels this deception by suggesting that it is hopeless to try to live a Christian life. The miracle of being made whole and living victoriously depends upon an individual believing that God loves him and is for him! The following scriptures declare this truth:

> Thou tellest my wanderings: put thou my tears into thy bottle: are they not in thy book? When I cry unto thee, then shall mine enemies turn back: this I know; for God is for me. (Psalm 56:8-9)

182

. . . If God be for us, who can be against us?
(Romans 8:31)

This is my commandment, That ye love one
another, as I have loved you. Greater love
hath no man than this, that a man lay down
his life for his friends. Ye are my friends, if
ye do whatsoever I command you.
(John 15:12-14)

God loves humanity and is willing to magnificently transform the greatest tragedies in life into something good. The following testimony is a perfect example of the transforming power of Christ's love to change a life of sadness into joy and a spirit of mourning into dancing (Psalm 30:11). Though my brother, Bob, had difficulty believing that God loved him and was for him, his testimony reveals the love and blessings that God gave to him that changed his life.

As a child, Bob was a tenderhearted young boy who cringed at the sight of an animal being hurt. I remember my mother telling me that Bob was very sensitive, a character trait which perhaps contributed to his vulnerability to criticism. Many circumstances led Bob to believe the deception that he was not very smart.

The stronghold of a negative self-esteem was fortified both by his own thoughts that he was *"stupid and couldn't do anything right"* and by the oppression of Satan. The Stronghold resulted in the self-defeating behaviors of neither being serious about nor applying himself in school. Marginally passing grades stood as a confirmation of the deception that he lacked intelligence. Attempts to gain the approval and respect of his peers opened the door of influence from peers who were on a downward spiral into sin.

At age 15, Bob began drinking alcohol with his friends. His marginally passing grades plummeted with the consequence of flunking ninth grade. He repeated ninth grade the following year and again his grades were so poor that he barely passed. The school counselor scheduled Bob for some aptitude testing and for an appointment with the school psychologist to discuss the test results. During this meeting, the psychologist explained that the test results demonstrated his ability to be successful at the current grade level and that it was within his ability to achieve a "B" average. Subsequent to this meeting, there were no further recommendations for any psychiatric evaluation or counseling.

Tenth grade was a repeat performance of ninth grade with below passing grades in all classes. In addition, his use of alcohol had increased. The high school principal called Bob into his office for academic counseling. The counsel he gave proved to add insult to injury. The principal said, *"You know Bob, some people will use their education to run businesses and some people will use their education to work, but you are going to be a ditch digger, so you might as well quit school now."* Taking the principal's advice, he quit school and began working a job as a farm hand in exchange for room and board.

At the age of 17, Bob and several friends decided to join the Navy as they thought that would be a "neat experience." After passing their physicals, they agreed to meet at the bus depot on a scheduled day so they would all leave together. Our father drove him to the depot where he would meet with his friends, but he was the only one who showed up. Even though our father tried to persuade Bob that he did not have to leave, Bob left alone on the bus that day. He interpreted his friends not being there with him as a cruel joke and imagined that they were getting a good laugh out of him being the only one who showed up.

The Navy proved to be another disappointing experience. The alcohol abuse continued along with the use of another substance called "White Cross" or Benzedrine. After two years of service, the substance abuse, in addition to other unacceptable behaviors, led to an undesirable discharge. A legal appeal was made on his behalf and the status of the undesirable discharge was changed to a general discharge under honorable conditions. Returning home, he became employed as a car salesman. Since his sales manner was affable, the job was profitable, but much of his income was spent on alcohol and drugs. His poor self-esteem deteriorated even more.

His drug and alcohol use increased over the next eight years, and toward the end of that time he began having stomach problems. Realizing his addiction to drugs was increasingly becoming more of a problem, he voluntarily entered a drug and alcohol treatment program.

While in the program, one of the other patients gave him some marijuana, but being determined to stay clean, he gave the marijuana to a program counselor. At the completion of the 21-day program, an exit interview was scheduled with a priest for encouragement and support. During this conversation the priest dozed off several times while Bob expressed his thoughts and fears concerning leaving the program. At the completion of the meeting the priest woke up to give his final words of reassurance: *"I would like to think that you are going to make it, but I really don't think you are going to make it."* One month after leaving the program, he returned to his previous habits of substance abuse. Another three years would pass before Bob would be introduced to the Bible and God in a way he had never experienced before.

Shortly after my conversion experience, I began witnessing to my family about repentance, baptism and receiving the Holy Ghost. The Word of God was discussed at every family gathering. Bob seemed interested, but did not respond outwardly in a positive manner and expressed skepticism about "speaking in tongues." We discussed the scriptures in the Bible that describe the actual phenomenon of receiving the gift of the Holy Ghost with the evidence of speaking in another language, and he believed the scriptures. A few months later he was baptized, though at the time I do not think he really understood the concept of repentance and subsequently, he did not receive the Holy Ghost after he was baptized. Another five years passed before Bob experienced that glorious gift. During those five years his life outwardly seemed to continue as before, but inwardly God was dealing with his heart and slowly his thought patterns were changing.

One experience that was the result of God's dealing with Bob occurred when he was 35. The desire to be free of his alcohol addiction increased to a level of desperation. Being employed as a truck driver at the time allowed him time to think and to pray. While driving the truck one day he was overcome with such a feeling of desperation to be free of his addiction to alcohol that he fervently prayed for God to help him quit drinking. Approximately one month later while on a trip to California, he began to experience symptoms associated with cirrhosis of the liver. He described the symptoms as follows: *"My skin turned yellow. I had pain in the upper right side of my abdomen and my whole body swelled up, even my face."*

When he arrived in California he went to visit our brother, Tim, who was in the Navy and stationed in San Diego. Bob looked so terrible that Tim didn't even recognize him. Tim, being very concerned about his condition, encouraged him to see a doctor, which Bob refused to do. A close friend of Bob's, who also was concerned about his health, discussed his symptoms with her physician along with giving the physician a history of Bob's alcohol abuse. The physician told her that the symptoms were indicative of the advanced stage of cirrhosis of the liver and that even if he quit drinking, he probably would not survive. When she told Bob what the physician had said, he determined to quit drinking and miraculously was able to quit. The reason I use the word "miraculously" is because I believe these events were an answer, not only to his own prayer, but also to the prayers being prayed by others on his behalf. The symptoms subsided, and though he did not drink alcohol anymore, he continued to use other substances.

Bob began going to church with Tim when he was 39 years old. He also attended a Bible study taught by the pastor of the church. After the third lesson of the Bible study, Bob repented and received the Holy Ghost. Again miraculously, he was delivered from all desire to use any street drugs or to smoke cigarettes, which was quite a miracle since he had a three-pack a day smoking habit.

The day after receiving the Holy Ghost, a friend came to visit and offered Bob some marijuana. Refusing the offer he said, *"I don't use that stuff any more because I have the Holy Ghost now."* When his friend asked him what the Holy Ghost was, Bob asked him if he could teach him a Bible study about the Holy Ghost experience. The next day he began teaching Bible studies to his friend and, thereafter, to anyone who was willing to listen or be taught. He was no longer being influenced by his friends; he was now influencing them.

Bob is now 63 and remains free of all addictions. Since beginning his walk with God, there have been many wonderful events and changes in his life. He is married and has two children, ages 19 and 4. The miracles have not stopped for Bob. A few years ago, Satan came to attack and tempt him to believe that God had not really forgiven all the sins he had committed before he was in the church. This attack was so forceful that he decided to pray to God for the assurance that his sins were forgiven. He asked God to give him the assurance needed by allowing him to have a daughter. As you might expect, Bob at age 59 became the proud father of a beautiful baby girl on September 14, 2000. The birth of this child was by divine appointment in answer to a prayer by God's child.

It is an undeniable fact that God loves Bob and is "for him." I am reminded through Bob's testimony of a passage of scripture which states, "For the eyes of the Lord run to and fro throughout the whole earth, to show himself strong in the behalf of them whose heart is perfect toward him. . . " (II Chronicles 16:9).

Jesus is Our Healer

In chapter one, "Wilt Thou Be Made Whole," there were several physical maladies discussed that are known to be common to people who have experienced long-term emotional instability. Most Christians realize that when they are physically tired or ill, Satan will take advantage of their weakened condition and assault their minds. Often, during a long-term illness an individual will become vulnerable to the influence of the oppressive spirit of depression. A physician's response to this condition would probably be to prescribe an antidepressant. However, in any of the above circumstances, Christians need to remember two things: Man is limited in his ability to cure or to heal, but Jesus is able to heal all of our diseases and to give us peace of mind. Jesus is our Great Physician as declared in the following scriptures:

> Bless The Lord, O my soul: and all that is within me, bless his holy name. Bless the Lord, O my soul and forget not all his benefits: Who forgiveth all thine iniquities; who healeth all thy diseases. (Psalm 103:1-3)

> But he was wounded for our transgressions, he was bruised for our iniquities: the chastisement of our peace was upon him; and with his stripes we are healed. (Isaiah 53:5)

As a testimony of God's ability to heal, comfort and deliver, I would like to relate the story of a friend of mine whom I have known for many years and who will be referred to as Amy. I first met this young lady when she attended our church as a visitor with her sister. As she entered the church that day, I noticed that although Amy had very attractive facial features, her pallor and expressionless countenance gave her face the appearance of a lifeless mask, much like the faces one would see in a wax museum. She walked slowly down the center aisle, and though she was young, her posture and gait resembled that of elderly woman. However, before leaving the church that day, a great change had taken place in Amy's life. She repented, was baptized in Jesus' name for the remission of her sins and was filled with the Spirit of God with the evidence of speaking in other tongues. She had entered the sanctuary resembling a figure of the walking dead, and left the sanctuary alive as a reborn child of God. There is no physician like our Great Physician. The following is her life story as told in her own words.

As far back as I can remember, even in the first grade, I had a very low self-esteem. I felt like nobody liked me and that I never really fit in. My father and mother divorced when I was five. I lived with my mother after their divorce. I continued to struggle with a low self-esteem and when I was 10 I took my first drink of alcohol while staying at my cousin's house. Her father was an alcoholic and we were not closely supervised so we took some of his beer and drank it. My mother remarried, and my stepfather and I had some personality conflicts as he was the "sergeant type." In seventh grade my girlfriend and I started taking street drugs like acid, speed and marijuana. And, of course, we still drank alcohol. When I was 12, I ran away from home and lived on the streets staying at my friend's houses or wherever I could find a place to sleep. During this time I was assaulted.

[At this time in her life, my friend entered the social service system where she would be involved in many "programs" in an attempt to help her overcome her emotional and substance abuse problems].

I was in and out of facilities and homes over the next five years including the children's home, juvenile center, foster homes, group homes, adolescent treatment programs and hospital psychiatric wards. There were times when I was suicidal and I remember one time I cut myself with a razor blade. Sometimes I would be returned to my mother's home. I got married when I was 18, and shortly after we were married my husband became abusive. I was pregnant five times during this marriage, but all of the pregnancies ended in miscarriages. Three of them were because of physical abuse. During this time in my life I quit using any drugs other than alcohol and marijuana. We were divorced after two years.

I was very depressed and when I was 21 I entered another alcohol treatment center. My psychiatrist wanted to start me on an antidepressant, but decided that I needed to be off the alcohol in order to determine what my psychiatric problems really were. After completing this program, I was started on an antidepressant. My medications were changed several times trying to find a medication that would help me.

I met and dated a man who I later married. I became pregnant and gave birth to a beautiful baby girl. I was still on several different antidepressants, but my depression became more and more severe. I was so oppressed that I couldn't take care of my daughter or even get out of bed except to go to the bathroom. My husband took care of our daughter. My psychiatrist explained to me that I had severe psychomotor retardation related to my depression, which accounted for my slowness and difficulty in performing activities or even walking. The only time I left the house was to go to my weekly appointments: one with my psychiatrist, another with my counselor and the weekly meetings that I attended at Alcoholics Anonymous and at Al-Anon. I would take the phone off the wall because I did not want to talk to anyone. Most of my time in bed, I watched TV. I started watching some religious programs, which got me thinking about God.

My sister had started going to church. She came over to visit and talked to me about God and prayed for me. She asked me to go to church with her. I went to church with her and when the minister finished preaching he asked if anyone wanted to be baptized. Some people near me asked me if I wanted to be baptized. I figured it wouldn't hurt, because I had tried everything else and nothing had helped. I got baptized and God filled me with the Holy Ghost. The only way I can express how I felt is to say that I felt really good. For the first time in my life I felt that I really knew Jesus and that He was alive.

My sister and I began taking a Bible study. At my next appointment with my psychiatrist I told him I had started going to church and did not need to see him any more as I was a Christian now. I stopped going to my counselor and the AA and Al-Anon meetings. Instead of going to my weekly appointments and meetings, I went to church three times a week and also continued the weekly Bible study.

I decided I needed to get off of the antidepressants. I stayed on them for about one month after I got the Holy Ghost, and then began to slowly decrease the doses as I weaned myself off of the medications. I know the Lord helped me make this decision and also to decide to gradually decrease the doses. While I was coming off of the antidepressants there were three times I was attacked by Satan and felt oppressed. I recognized the spiritual attack for what it was. For two years before I received the Holy Ghost, there was never a day that I did not feel severely depressed and after I got the Holy Ghost I was not depressed for about two weeks.

The first time I was depressed after getting the Holy Ghost, it only lasted approximately two weeks though it was very hard to go through. I just saturated myself in prayer and going to church. Satan attacked my mind, telling me that I would never get out of my depression, but I remembered that when I received the Holy Ghost I was totally free of depression for two weeks, so in my mind I fought against this lie and I came out of the depression.

The second time I became depressed it was a shorter episode and again I saturated myself with prayer. The depressed feeling was not as severe and didn't last as long as the first episode. The third episode lasted only a few days after which, I came out of the depression totally and have never been depressed again. It has been nineteen years now and I have been through many difficulties and trials, but I have continued to be free of depression.

Jesus is the Author and the Finisher of Our Faith

The word "author" has multiple meanings. As used in the preceding context, Jesus is the author or the "One that originates or gives existence: Source." Jesus is the source of a Christian's faith. The other meaning of the word author, "the writer of a literary work," could also be applicable in view of the association of Jesus with His body, the church. To fully understand the meaning of the statement that Jesus is the author and finisher of our faith we need to examine the following scriptures in Hebrews 12:1-3:

> Wherefore seeing we also are compassed about with so great a cloud of witnesses, let us lay aside every weight, and the sin which doth so easily beset us, and let us run with patience the race that is set before us, Looking unto Jesus the author and finisher of

our faith; who for the joy that was set before him endured the cross, despising the shame, and is set down at the right hand of the throne of God. For consider him that endured such contradiction of sinners against himself, lest ye be wearied and faint in your minds.

Jesus is the author or pioneer who blazed the trail before us and provided not only the sacrifice, but opened the way of salvation, making it possible for us to follow in His footsteps. We are reminded in the preceding scriptures, to consider what Jesus has done for us, to prevent us from becoming wearied or faint in our minds. In addition, Jesus has assured us that once we are filled with His Spirit and have become part of His body, there is nothing that shall separate us from the His love.

Who shall separate us from the love of Christ? shall tribulation, or distress, or persecution, or famine, or nakedness, or peril, or sword? As it is written, For thy sake we are killed all the day long; we are accounted as sheep for the slaughter. Nay, in all these things we are more than conquerors through him that loved us. For I am persuaded, that neither death, nor life, nor angels, nor principalities, nor powers, nor things present, nor things to come, Nor height, nor depth, nor any other creature, shall be able to separate us from the love of God, which is in Christ Jesus our Lord. (Romans 8:35-39)

Every Christian would benefit from letting these scriptures stand as a memorial in his mind. Jesus, as the author of our faith, ". . . was in all points tempted like as we are, yet without sin" (Hebrews 4:15). And, because of His own suffering in His body of flesh, He has compassion for us in our suffering. He further tells us to cast all of our cares upon Him because He cares for us (I Peter 5:7).

The second aspect of the meaning of the word "author" as "the writer of a literary work" is also applicable to the idea of the authorship of Christ in a Christian's life as portrayed in the following scriptures:

> Do we begin again to commend ourselves? or need we, as some others, epistles of commendation to you, or letters of commendation from you? Ye are our epistle written in our hearts, known and read of all men: Forasmuch as ye are manifestly declared to be the epistle of Christ ministered by us, written not with ink, but with the Spirit of the living God; not in tables of stone, but in fleshly tables of the heart. (II Corinthians 3:1-3)

I believe it would be acceptable to extract a two-fold meaning from the preceding scriptures in relation to Christ's authorship in the life of a Christian. Once born of Christ's Spirit, Jesus puts His laws into His child's mind and writes His laws on his heart (Hebrews 8:10). Men read a Christian's life as they would a book; and, hopefully, his actions reveal Christ to those around him. The second meaning of Christ's authorship in a Christian's life is derived from the submission of his life to the will of God. Jesus commands that we present our bodies as a living sacrifice, not being conformed to the world, but being transformed by the renewing of our minds that we might perform the good, acceptable and perfect will of God (Romans 12:1-2). As an author or writer, Jesus leads and guides a Christian's feet on paths which will become the chapters of his life. The end of that Christian's life, if it has been submitted to Christ, will allow him to join Jesus in the place He has prepared for him.

Jesus is not only the author, but He is the *finisher* of *our* faith. According to *Strong's Concordance* the word "finisher" means to bring to "completeness" [or] "perfection." Though it would seem impossible for a Christian in this life to achieve the level of perfection implied in the preceding definition, nevertheless, I do believe that we are to press toward that mark. The completion of Christ's work of faith and perfection in a Christian's life will be fully realized upon His return for His church, as revealed in I John 3:2: "Beloved, now are we the sons of God, and it doth not yet appear what we shall be: but we know that, when he shall appear, we shall be like him; for we shall see him as he is."

Christ's work as the author and finisher of a Christian's faith can be visualized in the testimony of a very close friend of mine whom I have known for more than eight years. This man, who henceforth will be referred to as John, is a man of faith. Though I know a great deal more of John's testimony than I am able to share in this chapter, I will try to present some of the highlights of the miraculous healing and deliverance that God worked in his life.

John became disillusioned with life when he was just a child. While telling me his life story he said, *"I suffered a deep wound in my heart because my father never loved me."* In addition to the feeling of not being loved, was the frequent verbal and physical abuse that he suffered at his father's hands. At age 14 John began to use both alcohol and marijuana on a frequent basis. He married at the age of 20 and moved 2000 miles away from his hometown to Texas. Though John loved his wife very much, they began having problems in their marriage related to his drug use. With the birth of their daughter, John had a greater desire to straighten out his life and save his marriage. Yet, he was unable to rid himself of his addictions. After five chaotic years of marriage, John's wife took their daughter and returned to her parents' home and shortly thereafter started divorce proceedings. John found the loss of his wife and daughter unbearable. Attempting to drown his sorrow, he began snorting cocaine, and with his addiction to this substance, entered another downward spiral into greater depths of sin and degradation. He became hooked on pornography, which led to the development of sexual perversions in his life. He frequented parties where people with bisexual lifestyles gathered to get high and have sex. Quickly, his life became consumed with parties, drugs and sex as he crossed the threshold into a bisexual lifestyle.

Around this time, John moved to California with no other goal in mind than to continue his current lifestyle. In California he met a woman to whom he was very attracted and, subsequently, desired to get out of the life of drugs, settle down, get married and have children. John married for the second time, but the demonic oppression in his life was greater than his own desire and ability to overcome the oppression. Instead of John joining his wife in her lifestyle, she joined him in his lifestyle of parties and drugs. During their first year of marriage, his wife became pregnant and gave birth to a baby girl. Again he struggled with the desire to change his life because he loved his daughter, but now he was a prisoner in his own body, addicted to drugs and oppressed by Satan. His addictions had progressed to smoking crack cocaine and taking crystal meth. Supporting his habits meant being involved in petty crimes, which landed him in jail several times over a period of two years for sentences of 30 to 60 days at a time.

At a party one night, John and his friends were using crack cocaine when suddenly he felt a sharp pain shoot down his side and immediately he fell to the floor flat on his face. Apparently, no one at the party seemed to notice he had fallen and if they did notice, they didn't care. He tried to turn over and found he was paralyzed on one side of his body and unable to speak. Struggling, he managed to turn to his side and attempted to get someone's attention, but no one responded. A little while later his "friends" decided to leave as they thought he was dying and were concerned, for themselves, that there might be legal ramifications surrounding his death. Stepping over him on their way to the door, one of his "friends" took his money. Fortunately, they left the door ajar and a short time later a woman walking by saw the door ajar and looked in. When she saw John lying on the floor, she called for an ambulance. He had suffered a stroke and for the next two months would continue to have weakness and stiffness on the right side of his body. Gradually, he recovered his strength and mobility.

John's world was about to come crashing down around him. His wife had become totally disillusioned with their marriage and though she was pregnant with their second child she began seeing another man. Finances were low as John was only working side jobs here and there. He had started working for a man who owned a motel and on one particular day he was unloading some heavy oak doors off a truck. The man standing in the truck pushed three of the doors toward him at one time. When he caught the doors, he sank to his knees under the heavy load, immediately feeling intense pain in his lower abdomen and groin area. Physically, John was already very emaciated and weak because for the previous two weeks he had been on a crack run, meaning that he had been taking crack every day for the last two weeks and had not eaten any food. Though he was in intense pain, he somehow managed to walk home, a distance of two blocks.

Upon entering their apartment, he found his wife with another man. They were in the process of packing and about to leave. His wife, wanting to avoid any resistance from him, immediately called the police. Upon their arrival, she told the police that John had physically abused her. Subsequently he was arrested and taken to jail. While being frisked by a guard, he cried out in pain. The guard lifted his shirt and saw several large lumps or hernias in John's lower abdomen and groin areas. Immediately he was taken to the emergency room at the nearest hospital.

As he lay on a gurney in the emergency room, a physician came over to examine him. The physician had just examined the man next to him and John overheard the physician say to the nurse, *"Get the other man ready for emergency surgery as that one* [referring to John] *isn't going to make it."* When the same physician returned a few hours later, he found that John was still alive. The physician examined him again and asked him to sign a consent form to have emergency surgery, which he refused to sign. The doctor looking intently at him, asked him, *"Do you have a mother or father or any children or anyone that you ever want to see again and would be willing to live for?"* Thinking of his two daughters and the baby soon to be born, he agreed to sign the consent form. He was taken to surgery and did not regain consciousness the rest of that day. The next day he awoke in a private room with a guard in uniform standing outside his hospital room door. He found out latter that the physician who had performed the surgery had paid for his private room and also had not charged any fees for the surgery he had performed. When John was stable and could be transferred, he was taken to the medical ward at the County jail where he remained for one month before being transferred to the general population area of the jail.

During his month's stay in the medical ward there was an orderly who prayed for John every day. His recovery was slow because of his malnourished condition and his withdrawal from the drugs. For the first two weeks in the medical ward, he had hallucinations related to withdrawal from the drugs. After the hallucinations subsided, the orderly, who had been faithfully praying for him, began to read the *Bread of Life* publication to him every day. God was dealing with John's heart and faith was being instilled in his mind. [Paul stated in Romans 10:17 that ". . . faith cometh by hearing, and hearing by the word of God"]. After one month in the medical ward, John was transferred to the general population area of the jail where he completed the remaining time of his 45-day sentence for spousal abuse.

While in the general population area of the jail, an inmate approached him and said that he felt led by God to read the *Gospel of John* to him. Again he was hearing the Word of God and the Word was changing his heart. John also came in contact with some ministers who visited the jail and through them he heard about the Christian Men's

Home, a group home that he entered when he was released from jail. Over a six-month period while in this home, he continued to read the Bible. He was particularly intrigued with scriptures pertaining to receiving the gift of the Holy Ghost. Three months after arriving at the group home, John decided he wanted the Holy Ghost and went down to the basement alone to pray. A short time later, he started speaking in tongues, and he knew that he had received the Holy Ghost.

Directly across the street from the group home was a mission that was funded and managed by the Christian Life Center Church. The mission gave free food and clothing to anyone in need. John started working at the mission in exchange for food and clothing to be given to the Christian Men's Home. One of the ministers at the mission taught him a Bible study about the deity of Jesus Christ and the importance of being baptized in Jesus' name. John focused his reading and study of the Bible in the Book of Acts and received a revelation of his need to be baptized in Jesus' name for the remission of his sins. After he graduated from the program at the Christian Men's Home, he began attending the Christian Life Center Church in Stockton, California, and shortly thereafter was baptized in the name of Jesus. That was in 1993, and John continues to attend that church.

Currently, he serves in the work of God as a lay minister, and his main ministry has been working with new converts and teaching Bible studies to men and women in drug and alcohol treatment centers. John has been free of his drug addiction and the oppression of Satan since the Lord began to minister to him through the prayers of the orderly in the medical ward of the jail. Looking back over the years, he is able to testify that Jesus is the author and finisher of his faith.

John has experienced many miracles, blessings and victories. One of the greatest blessings was that of gaining sole physical custody of his two youngest daughters. All three of his daughters have been baptized in Jesus' name and the two oldest are both filled with the Holy Ghost.

The Promise is Unto You and To Your Children

Our society seems to be unaware of the spiritual forces of good and evil that operate within our nation and our world. The lack of knowledge regarding the spiritual realm and its influence on human thinking and behavior may be in part due to the redefining of what our culture considers righteous or evil. Most Americans do not equate sin or evil with what the Bible declares sin to be. And, there seems to be an unspoken attitude that one should not speak or teach about the evil influence of Satan in relation to children's behavior. However, Christians realize that children are influenced by both good and evil as evidenced by the following scriptures:

> But continue thou in the things which thou has learned and hast been assured of, knowing of whom thou has learned them; And that from a child thou has known the holy scriptures, which are able to make thee wise unto salvation through faith which is in Christ Jesus. All scripture is given by inspiration of God, and is profitable for doctrine, for reproof, for correction, for instruction in righteousness. (II Timothy 3:14-16)

And when they were come to the multitude, there came to him a certain man, kneeling down to him, and saying, Lord, have mercy on my son: for he is lunatick, and sore vexed: for ofttimes he falleth into the fire, and oft into the water. And I brought him to thy disciples, and they could not cure him. Then Jesus answered and said, O faithless and perverse generation, how long shall I be with you? how long shall I suffer you? bring him hither to me. And Jesus rebuked the devil; and he departed out of him: and the child was cured from that very hour. Then came the disciples to Jesus apart, and said, Why could not we cast him out? And Jesus said unto them, Because of your unbelief: for verily I say unto you, If ye have faith as a grain of mustard seed, ye shall say unto this mountain, Remove hence to yonder place; and it shall remove; and nothing shall be impossible unto you. Howbeit this kind goeth not out but by prayer and fasting. (Matthew 17:14-21)

When children are exposed to good or evil influences, their minds are affected by those influences. The following testimony was told to me by a very close friend of mine whose son, Ryan, was started on Ritalin at a young age because of his behavior problems.

As a young child, Ryan was almost fearless. Things that would scare other children his age did not frighten him. Also he was not able to connect his undesirable behaviors with the consequences of those behaviors. Ryan's mother,

Rachel, described her son as being a very active child who was restless at times. Ryan started kindergarten shortly after turning six. Early in the school year, his teacher notified Rachel that Ryan's behavior was disruptive to both her and the class. He had difficulty sitting still and would frequently talk out of turn. The teacher noticed that he also had difficulty staying on task with his activities more so than the other children. Approximately halfway through the year, he was started on Ritalin. Ryan told his mother he didn't like the way Ritalin made him feel. He experienced side effects of headaches and decreased appetite. His mother stated, *"There was no significant improvement in his behavior after starting the Ritalin."*

First grade was a repeat of kindergarten and he continued to have the same type of behavioral problems, despite the continued use of Ritalin. Ryan's academic achievement was poor. In reading and math and in his social skills he received a "needs improvement." All other activities or subjects were graded as "satisfactory." Though he passed first grade in the public school, Rachel decided to enroll him in a Christian school the following year for two reasons. First, she had always wanted him to be in a Christian school and secondly, she preferred the academic curriculum that was used in the Christian school to that used in the public schools.

After being tested at the Christian school, the counselor recommended that Ryan repeat the first grade and Rachel agreed that this would be best for her son. Ryan's behavior and academic achievement, however, continued to be a problem. His teacher was sensitive to his needs and spent time every day working one-on-one with him to help him learn what was being taught. His teacher understood the influence that God's Spirit has on children and, therefore, each school day was started with prayer. One morning in the early part of January, there was a wonderful presence of God in the classroom as the children prayed, and Ryan became very earnest in his praying. The other children were encouraged to pray with him, and after a short time of praying, he received the gift of the Holy Ghost speaking with other tongues. Thereafter, both his teacher and his mother noticed a significant change in his behavior.

His ability to focus increased and he was able to complete his schoolwork; consequently his grades improved. Approximately one month after receiving the Holy Ghost, Rachel began slowly weaning him off the Ritalin. After another month, the Ritalin was completely stopped and his behavior continued to improve as well as his grades. By the end of the year he was getting "A's" and "B's" in all his subjects. The only behavior that seemed to be an ongoing struggle was talking during class, which was not viewed as an abnormal behavior for an eight-year-old. Since I was closely acquainted with both Ryan and his mother during this three-year period of his life, I can attest to the above testimony and the changes that took place in Ryan's life after receiving the Holy Ghost. The power and influence of the Spirit of God in any individual's life brings a dynamic change, regardless of his or her age.

The subtitle that introduced this section of the chapter was taken from Acts 2:39. Peter, preaching in Jerusalem on the day of Pentecost just after he and many others had received the gift of the Holy Ghost, described to the crowd how they could receive that same experience and be saved.

> Then Peter said unto them, Repent, and be
> baptized everyone of you in the name of Jesus
> Christ for the remission of sins, and ye shall

receive the gift of the Holy Ghost. For the promise is unto you, and to your children, and to all that are afar off, even as many as the Lord our God shall call. And with many other words did he testify and exhort, saying, Save yourselves from this untoward generation. Then they that gladly received his word were baptized: and the same day there were added unto them about three thousand souls. (Acts 2:38-41)

According to the preceding scriptures it is clear that the gift of the Holy Ghost is promised to children as well as to adults. Knowing God can work miracles in our children's lives is a tremendous comfort. Believing these scriptures, we can pray in faith for our children and be assured that God will save and deliver them from sin and oppression. I have personally witnessed the miracle-working power of the Holy Ghost in perhaps hundreds of children and adolescents over the last 30 years that I have been in the church. The precious Holy Ghost experience allows all people to be delivered from sin and spiritual oppression.

God is Not the Author of Confusion

"For God is not the author of confusion, but of peace..." (I Corinthians 14:33). The apostle Paul writing to the church in Corinth was instructing the church on the orderly execution of the gift of tongues and interpretation for apparently two reasons: to avoid disorder in the services and to prevent any confusion in the minds of visitors, who hearing the tongues might become confused and think the church members were mad [crazy] (I Corinthians 14). The precept that God is not the author of confusion, but of peace is applicable when considering that a sound mind or a disciplined mind is not a confused or disordered mind. A state of mental confusion is not the result of God's influence upon a person's mind, but there is a correlation between confusion and evil as evidenced by the following scriptures:

> Who is a wise man and endued with knowledge among you? let him shew out of a good conversation his works with meekness of wisdom. But if ye have bitter envying and strife in your hearts, glory not, and lie not against the truth. This wisdom descendeth not from above, but is earthly, sensual, devilish. For where envying and strife is, there is confusion and every evil work. But the wisdom that is from above is first pure, then peaceable, gentle, and easy to be intreated, full of mercy and good fruits, without partiality, and without hypocrisy. And the fruit of righteousness is sown in peace of them that make peace. (James 3:13-18)

Confusion is another form of spiritual oppression. Most emotionally unstable people report that they suffer from confusion, which affects their lives in many ways. One individual I have known for many years suffered from such a degree of confusion that it was difficult, and at times impossible, for her to function either socially or in an employment capacity. I was privileged to teach her about the promises of deliverance, healing and salvation through the *Search for Truth* Bible study. For approximately two years we spent a great deal of time together studying the Scriptures. The following testimony will be a joint effort in her words and mine.

Jennifer told me that as a child she was quiet and introverted, not wanting to go outside and play with other children, but rather to stay inside and be with her mom. She felt like she didn't fit in anywhere; this was also true in school. Apparently, when she was about eight she began to think she was different from other children. With this realization came a change in her perception of herself. She said, *"I came to the conclusion that there was something wrong with me."*

Another family circumstance that contributed to her fear, confusion and poor self-esteem was her relationship with her father, who was an alcoholic. Often, he would stay out drinking until the early morning hours and after returning home, he would proceed to wake up everyone in the house. Jennifer was always tired in school because of her sleep being interrupted, which resulted in a decline in her academic performance. She described her emotional state at age ten as follows:

My anxiety and fears, as I think back, were related to the constant upheaval in our home. My family never knew what tomorrow would bring as my father often became violent when he was drinking. It got to the point that if my father was out late drinking, my mother would take us [the children] *and we would go to the Drive-Inn Theater. When we left there, we would all just sleep in the car until we knew dad was gone and then we would go home.*

Jennifer was gradually becoming more fearful and confused about her own behaviors. In her attempt to understand herself, she became very self-focused. She was painfully aware that other people also viewed her as "different." She stated, *"My sister's friends would ask my sisters, 'Why doesn't she ever talk?' I was afraid of people and tried to figure out why I was afraid and why I didn't act like other people."*

At the age of 13, Jennifer's father and mother divorced. After their divorce she became even more introverted and also started to gain weight. Frequently, she felt anxious, a feeling that was usually accompanied by pain in her stomach. Her mother was concerned about the abdominal pain and scheduled an appointment with a physician. The physician did not seem overly concerned about her physical or emotional condition. Jennifer continued to have problems in school and finally when she was sixteen, she decided to quit school. Her older sister invited Jennifer to live with them and to help with the care of her niece, who was a newborn baby.

While living with her sister, the episodes of abdominal pain became more severe and consequently she was seen by another physician. During this visit she expressed her fear that she was going to die. The physician informed her that further tests were needed to determine the cause of her stomach problems, which would necessitate her being hospitalized. In addition, he ordered some psychological testing. Apparently, he was more concerned about her emotional state than he was about her physical state because when she arrived at the hospital she was admitted to the locked ward of the psych unit. While on this unit, she met with a psychologist several times a week and a psychiatrist once a week. Jennifer described her stay in the hospital as follows:

During one of the first group therapy sessions, I observed the psychologist as he talked with another girl in the group. His approach was like an interrogation, and she started crying. I made up my mind right then that I was going to remain silent and that he was not going to be able to do that to me. After my second meeting with the psychiatrist, he told me that it was no longer necessary for me to be in the hospital and that I could be seen as an outpatient. They did not find any medical reason for my stomach problems. While I was in the hospital they offered me medications to help my emotions and to help me sleep, but I never wanted to take any kind of medications so I refused to take them.

Jennifer wanted to accomplish something with her life. She said, *"I wanted to do something with my life, but I didn't know what to do. My stepmother encouraged me to take the GED. I studied for the test and passed it. Then I decided I wanted to take some college courses, but to support myself, I had to hold down two jobs leaving no time for college."* One of her jobs was working as a bartender and drinking quickly became a problem. She also began experimenting with some other drugs, which she continued to do between the ages of 18-30. During these years, her anxiety, fear, confusion and depression continued, but the anxiety was the most difficult for her to endure. She described the anxiety attacks as follows:

There were times when I would have anxiety attacks and would not be able to do anything. I kept trying to talk myself out of my anxiety and fears and would try to analyze why I thought and felt the way I did. My times of anxiety and depression were becoming more frequent. Another emotional problem that developed was anger. I was very confused about my purpose in life and just about life in general. When I was 30 my sister met a woman at her work, who was going to be teaching her a Bible study and my sister asked me if I wanted to be involved.

210

The next section of this testimony will be my observations of Jennifer during the time I taught her and her sisters a Bible study. My first meeting with Jennifer took place at the house she shared with her friend. When she answered the door, I immediately recognized the mask of hopelessness and despair that I knew she would refer to as depression. She was also suffering from anxiety and confusion, almost to a point of distraction. As she offered explanations about needing to clean the house, I reflected on the typical behavior of many emotionally crippled individuals who are unable to manage even the regular tasks of daily living. The house was in need of cleaning and organizing, and though not cluttered to the degree of leaving only pathways, it was not far from that condition. This observation is not meant as a criticism, rather it demonstrates the debilitating effects that oppression may engender in an individual's life.

During the first two or three Bible studies, Jennifer was very quiet—not commenting or asking questions. This behavior was to be expected since she had not yet learned to trust me. Weeks passed and as our Bible studies continued she gradually began to open up to me. Many comments about herself or her life circumstances in general were prefaced by statements such as, *"I just don't know why. . . "* or *"I am so confused about. . . ."* She was very interested in the Bible and readily received it as the Word of God and as truth. When discussing scriptures, she would often respond in a tone of relief saying, *"That makes sense,"* or *"I believe that. . . ."* Her confusion concerning the thoughts and ideas she had previously formed about life and herself seemed less puzzling to her in light of the Scriptures. The weekly Bible studies were very important to her and I realized by her comments that she waited with great anticipation for the next Bible study. God was becoming real to her in a way that she had not known Him before. Many of her ideas and concepts about the character of God were false, such as the thought that He was punishing her for things that were out of her control.

Studying the Word of God, coupled with God's gentle leading helped her to think differently and with the change in her thoughts came changes in her life. Shortly after she started going to church, she faced her first major decision. The man she was living with was not her husband and she knew that she needed to either marry or move out of his house. She was afraid to embark on either of those actions because she felt confused and did not want to do anything wrong. After thinking more about this, she realized that she felt both the conviction that the relationship was wrong according to the Word of God, and that she needed to move. Her focus from that time forward was to obey the Word of God and any decisions that would be made would be in agreement with the Scriptures. Prior to her moving out of her friend's house another event occurred that confirmed her need to move quickly and to follow through on what she knew she needed to do to be saved. This event took place the night her sister was baptized.

Although Jennifer thought it was too soon for herself to be baptized, she wanted to be with her sister when she was baptized. Leaving the church that night, she turned a corner and saw headlights coming out of the ditch on the opposite side of the road heading directly toward her car. She pulled over to the right shoulder of the road but the lights continued advancing toward her car. Quickly she drove up onto the embankment and yet the lights continued in her direction. The car did not seem to be slowing as it approached. Realizing a collision was imminent, she quickly exited the car and simultaneously she felt peace. The oncoming car somehow came to a stop within three feet of her car. The woman in the other car was laughing and appeared intoxicated. A police car appeared and the policeman got out of his car and walked toward the other car. Jennifer's sister, who had been following Jennifer in her own car, ran up to her to make sure she was all right. Jennifer's immediate comment to her sister was to tell her that she was going to be baptized right away. She moved out of her friend's house, moved in with her sister and a few days later was baptized.

Her testimony about the experience of receiving the Holy Ghost is as follows:

While taking the Bible study I realized that I needed to obey the Scriptures. Though I didn't get the Holy Ghost right after getting baptized I believed I would soon get it, as it was a promise in the Bible. One night, approximately three months later, I received the Holy Ghost while I was just worshiping God.

The Word of God helped me to realize how oppressed I was in my thinking. The Lord began to talk to me about how I did not have to go through this kind of oppression. Even after receiving the Holy Ghost the devil tried to torment me and to take me back into the bondage of confusion, depression, anxiety and fear. I was having emotional highs and lows; these mood swings were terrible. Each time this happened I cried out to God to help me and then I would feel relief.

There were two things that brought what I considered to be a severe spiritual attack from Satan against me. The first thing was reading the Bible. Every time I read the Bible I would become very anxious. I was desperate to know the Word of God and to find something in the Bible that could help me, but I would become so anxious that I wasn't able to keep reading until I found a scripture that helped me. I bought a Bible promise book, a book of scriptures that could encourage someone going through problems such as fear, anxiety or loneliness. This book opened the door for me to be able to read the Bible. What I learned from the scriptures in the Bible promise book was what I was supposed to think.

The second thing the devil wanted to stop in my life was my going to church. Whenever I was in church I would become anxious. The anxiety would increase until I felt like I couldn't stand it any longer. During these times, I would be confused about whether I was being convicted or whether the anxiety was due to guilt. In this state of mind, I would get up and leave church. One of the people in the church talked to me about my problem and explained that my leaving church is exactly what Satan wanted because the preaching of the Word of God would help me to overcome the anxiety. I believed this statement and made up my mind to stay in church no matter how anxious I felt. I did exactly that and the preached Word of God was so powerful that I got all the help I needed whether it was direction, comfort, healing or deliverance.

One Sunday when there was a guest evangelist preaching, the Lord revealed to the evangelist that I was oppressed and the ministers prayed for me. As they prayed I felt a release from the oppression.

During another sermon, I realized that I needed to give my thinking and my mind to God. The preacher explained that we needed to gird up the loins of our mind with the Word of God so God could establish our thoughts. I finally understood that my analytical thinking was causing me trouble. As I flooded my mind with the Word of God I was able to give up my analytical thinking and establish my thoughts according to the Word of God. I also realized at that time that I still really didn't know who I was, but I did know who I was not and I knew that Jesus would make something wonderful out of my life. I knew He would give purpose to my life.

Another problem I had was, I didn't have very many friends. It wasn't until years later that I realized why it was so difficult for people to be around me. Not only was I moody, I was also sullen and angry. My sister and the people in the church who were spiritually mature didn't give up on me. My sister had faith in God and because of her faith in God she had faith in me. God helped me to know that He wanted to be my best friend and that He didn't want me to be dependent upon a person, but rather on Him. God taught me that as I drew closer to Him making Him my best friend, then He would help me to develop other friendships.

As God did these miracles in my life I became more and more even-keeled in my emotions and I felt whole. The key to being whole and maintaining that wholeness is accomplished by being faithful to God and maintaining an inward hunger for a relationship with Him. Whenever I face a difficult time I go back to my commitment of giving my whole self to Him because I am dependent on Him. It is like the relationship a child has with his parents; the child is able to be carefree because he knows his parents will take care of his problems.

My life now is like a fairy tale. I have a wonderful Christian husband and companion and I realize through my marriage relationship that God is always trying to show me how much He loves me. Because of my journey with the Lord, I have been able to minister to others, so now I have a definite purpose in life. My advice to other people is: When you don't understand, just take hold of His hand.

The testimonies of people who have been comforted, healed and delivered from the oppression and the bondage of sin are unending. Every day there are individuals who are receiving God's miracles, healing and deliverance in their lives. The list of the "nuggets of truth" that will become mind-sets for victory in a Christian's life is also unending. For every problem or need that a Christian may face, God has an answer and a promise!

Chapter Sixteen

Forgive and Ye Shall be Forgiven

Of all the "nuggets of truth" that God has revealed to me since I received the Holy Ghost, there is none more precious than the truth that will be discussed in this chapter. I pray that each person reading this chapter will allow this truth to prosper in his life as it has in mine.

Chapters six and seven of the Book of Acts record the story of Stephen, who the Bible declares to be, ". . . a man full of faith and of the Holy Ghost" and who through faith and the power of the Holy Ghost ". . . did great wonders and miracles among the people." Stephen was accused of having spoken blasphemous words against Moses and against God. Because of these false accusations that were made against him, he was brought before the Sanhedrin (Jewish Court). In answer to the accusations, he gave brief accounts of the lives of Abraham, Joseph and Moses, bringing the listeners historically to the time when the children of Israel refused to obey Moses and persuaded Aaron to make an idol for them to worship as their god. Stephen reminded all those, before whom he now stood, of other incidents when their fathers worshiped false gods. He concluded his discourse with the following statements:

Ye stiffnecked and uncircumcised in heart and ears, ye do always resist the Holy Ghost: as your fathers did, so do ye. Which of the prophets have not your fathers persecuted? and they have slain them which shewed before of the coming of the Just One; of whom ye have been now the betrayers and murderers: Who have received the law by the disposition of angels, and have not kept it. (Acts 7:51-53)

Acts 7:54-60 records the account of the actions of those who heard Stephen's words and his response to their actions:

When they heard these things, they were cut to the heart, and they gnashed on him with their teeth. But he, being **full of the Holy Ghost**, looked up stedfastly into heaven, and saw the glory of God, and Jesus standing on the right hand of God, And said, Behold, I see the heavens opened, and the Son of man standing on the right hand of God. Then they cried out with a loud voice, and stopped their ears, and ran upon him with one accord, And cast him out of the city, and stoned him: and the witnesses laid down their clothes at a young man's feet, whose name was Saul. And they stoned Stephen, calling upon God, and saying, Lord Jesus, receive my spirit. And he kneeled down, and cried with a loud voice, **Lord, lay not this sin to their charge.** And when he had said this, he fell asleep.

The preceding verses of scripture portray several things about Stephen. He was "fully yielded" to the Spirit of God and that was the determining factor guiding his response when he was confronted with false accusations, unfair judgment and even the acts of violence against him, which resulted in his death. Stephen's actions and words reveal the surrender of his will and his life to the divine nature and will of Christ in him. In his suffering and in his death, he demonstrated the sacrificial love of God. He was willing to give his life, and he was willing to forgive as he prayed that God would pardon the actions of those who murdered him. Stephen's words and actions were very similar to those of Jesus when He gave His life. As recorded in Luke 23:34, while Jesus was on the cross, He said, "Father, forgive them; for they know not what they do." And in the same chapter, verse 46, Jesus cried with a loud voice and said, "Father, into thy hands I commend my spirit."

Christians realize that Jesus gave His life so that their sins could be forgiven. He, in turn, commands that we are to follow His example and to forgive those who trespass against us. Although it may seem relatively easy at times to forgive, there are other times and circumstances when forgiving seems difficult, if not impossible. Emotionally crippled individuals who may have suffered repeated and long-term verbal and/or physical abuse may find it difficult to forgive their abusers. Other individuals have had to endure seeing someone they love being hurt, or perhaps they have even suffered the loss of a loved one at the hands of another individual. Even Christians find it difficult under these circumstances to forgive those who have committed such acts. Yet, Jesus commands Christians to forgive and has linked their salvation to the obedience of this commandment:

> And when ye stand praying, forgive, if ye have ought against any: that your Father also which is in heaven may forgive you your trespasses. But if ye do not forgive, neither will your Father which is in heaven forgive your trespasses. (Mark 11:25-26)

Salvation alone is not the only thing that will be determined by whether a Christian forgives those who trespass against him; his emotional, physical and spiritual well-being are likewise at stake. A Christian's peace of mind is closely linked to forgiving others. Another question to be considered is: Once God has delivered an individual from an emotionally crippled state, what would protect or prevent that individual from becoming emotionally crippled again? The answer to this question lies in fully understanding the meaning of forgiveness.

People usually associate the word "forgive" with the meaning "to excuse" or to "to cease to feel resentment against" someone who has offended or hurt them. Forgive is also defined as to cancel a debt or an obligation owed by another person. However, there is another meaning for the word "forgive" that brings a greater dimension to the concept of forgiving.

In reference to the New Testament only, there are 58 times that the word "forgive," or a form of the word "forgive," appears. In 57 of the 58 scriptures, forgive has been translated from the Greek word "aphiemi" which means to send, remit, put away, or lay aside (*Strong's Concordance*). However, in Luke 6:37, the Greek word "apoluo," which was translated as forgive, means "to free fully" or to "release" (*Strong's Concordance*). According to Luke 6:37, Christians are admonished to, "Judge not, and ye shall not be judged: condemn not, and ye shall not be condemned: forgive, and ye shall be forgiven." It is difficult to grasp the complete meaning of Luke 6:37 without examining the context in which these words are recorded:

> But I say unto you which hear, Love your enemies, do good to them which hate you,
>
> Bless them that curse you, and pray for them which despitefully use you.
>
> And unto him that smiteth thee on the one cheek offer also the other; and him that taketh away thy cloak forbid not to take thy coat also.
>
> Give to every man that asketh of thee; and of him that taketh away thy goods ask them not again.
>
> And as ye would that men should do to you, do ye also to them likewise.
>
> For if ye love them which love you, what thank have ye? for sinners also love those that love them.

And if ye do good to them which do good to you, what thank have ye? for sinners also do even the same.

And if ye lend to them of whom ye hope to receive, what thank have ye? for sinners also lend to sinners, to receive as much again.

But love ye your enemies, and do good, and lend, hoping for nothing again; and your reward shall be great, and ye shall be the children of the Highest: for he is kind unto the unthankful and to the evil.

Be ye therefore merciful, as your Father also is merciful.

Judge not, and ye shall not be judged: condemn not, and ye shall not be condemned: forgive, and ye shall be forgiven:

Give, and it shall be given unto you; good measure, pressed down, and shaken together, and running over, shall men give unto your bosom. For with the same measure that ye mete withal it shall be measured to you again. (Luke 6:27-38)

The preceding scriptures seem to represent the epitome of perfect Christian character and behavior, which one should strive to attain, but may find very difficult to fully achieve. Nevertheless, Jesus does not view these attributes as unattainable, but challenges His children that as He is perfect, so they should be perfect (Matthew 5:48). Attaining these desirable attributes depends upon being, as Stephen was, "full of faith and of the Holy Ghost." Stephen's view of his circumstances and his reaction to his persecutors was not a product of his carnal mind. Instead, he chose to allow the Spirit of God in him to be his guide, therefore fulfilling the law of God.

> . . . Thou shalt love the Lord thy God with all thy heart, and with all thy soul, and with all thy mind. This is the first and great commandment. And the second is like unto it, Thou shalt love thy neighbor as thy self. On these two commandments hang all the law and the prophets. (Matthew 22:37-39)

True forgiveness in a Christian's heart involves more than just excusing or ceasing to feel resentment against an individual who has wronged him. There is the matter of **releasing** both the judgment and condemnation of that person to God. Forgiveness, according to Luke 6:37, means relinquishing the right to judge the intent, motive or behavior of another person. A Christian must surrender to God what he believes to be the evidence that condemns another person. God alone knows all of the evidence that would determine one's guilt or innocence. In addition, a Christian must realize that any resulting retribution must likewise remain in God's hands as He is a God of justice.

My last testimony in this book will serve to answer the question asked earlier in this chapter: Once God has delivered an individual from an emotionally crippled state, what would protect or prevent that individual from becoming emotionally crippled again?

Several years ago, a series of circumstances occurred that threatened to destroy my peace of mind. The emotional pain I endured during this time in my life, has allowed me to categorize that trial as a "fiery trial."

> Beloved, think it not strange concerning the fiery trial which is to try you, as though some strange thing happened unto you: But rejoice, inasmuch as ye are partakers of Christ's sufferings; that, when his glory shall be revealed, ye may be glad also with exceeding joy. (I Peter 4:12-13)

In the midst of the fiery trial, while feeling overwhelming desperation, I called a close friend and explained the circumstances I was experiencing. In almost a pleading manner I asked her, *"Will I ever be free from being able to be hurt like this again?"* She didn't respond immediately, but after a pause she said, *"I don't usually say that I have heard from God, but when you asked me that question, an answer immediately came into my mind and I believe this answer is from God."* She continued, *"The only way you will ever be free from being able to be hurt, is to **release** to God what was done in the past, what is happening now and anything that may happen in the future."* I knew that God had given her that answer for me.

I hung up the phone and cried out to God asking Him to help me to release everything to Him: the hurts of the past and present, and any hurts that may come to me in the future. The urgency of my prayer was equal to the desperation in my mind. The prayer was not lengthy, however, when I finished praying I felt a peace in my mind and spirit. Only time would reveal the extent of the miracle that began that day and has continued to work in my life in answer to that prayer. The revelation of forgive, meaning "to free fully" or to "release" came as a progressive revelation culminating in a greater depth of understanding as I wrote this chapter.

Releasing or surrendering one's will and judgment in favor of God's will and judgment gives birth to another miracle. By obeying the commandment given in Luke 6:37, to judge not, condemn not and to forgive (release); a Christian secures his own release from "emotional pain or crippling." He is set "fully free" from the bondage or oppression that he would have experienced because of his unwillingness to forgive. There is a tremendous comfort in knowing that because we have God's Spirit in us, we do not have to be vulnerable to oppression. This is not to imply that we will never experience emotional pain related to the actions of others, but we do not have to live with that pain. God has given us, through His Spirit, the power to be victorious over all emotional afflictions that accompany the difficult circumstances in life.

Stephen's response to those who stoned him is a perfect example of the spiritual freedom and victory forgiveness brings to a Christian's life. Though it was obvious that those who stoned him intended to kill him, he did not judge and condemn them for their actions. Instead, he cried out to God on their behalf, "Lord, lay not this sin to their charge" (Acts 7:60).

Over the years, there have been numerous times since I prayed that prayer asking God to help me release the hurts of the past, present and future, that I have had to surrender to God anew the memory of those hurts. Even as recently as this morning before working on this chapter, something had rekindled the memory of those circumstances that led me to pray that prayer. With the memory came a sadness, but a still small voice inside of me posed this question. *Why are you thinking about that?* Immediately and even without praying, in my mind I said, *I have already released that to you, God.* The memory and the emotions were gone as I cast those cares back upon Him.

I believe my testimony corresponds with the teaching of Jesus in Luke 6:37. Through forgiveness, I have secured my own "release" from the vulnerability of becoming spiritually oppressed or emotionally crippled. I am able to live in the realm of the promise of God that ". . . [He] hath not given us the spirit of fear; but of power and of love, and of a sound mind" (II Timothy 1:7).

Dear Reader,

I am praying that this book will be a blessing to you and a resource for you as you minister to others. If this book has helped you in any way, I would appreciate hearing from you at my email address. Ordering copies of the book may also be done online via Day Star Publications website.

Sincerely, Dale Anderson

To order *Breaking The Yoke Of Spiritual Oppression*
Go to: www.daystarpublications.com

You may contact the author via email at:
danderson@daystarpublications.com

Bibliography

Armstrong, Thomas. *The Myth of the A.D.D. Child: 50 Ways to Improve Your Child's Behavior and Attention Span Without Drugs, Labels, or Coercion.* 1995. New York: Plume, 1997.

Breggin, Peter R., and David Cohen. *Your Drug May Be Your Problem: How and Why to Stop Taking Psychiatric Medications.* Cambridge: Da Capo, 1999.

Brown, S. Avery, and John Loengard. "Miracle Worker." *People* magazine 15 November (1993): 153-155.

De Becker, Gavin. *The Gift Of Fear: Survival Signals That Protect Us From Violence.* Boston: Little, 1997.

Flick, Deborah L. *From Debate To Dialogue: Using the Understanding Process to Transform Our Conversations.* Boulder: Orchid, 1998.

Gorbachev, Mikhail S. "My Partner, the Pope." *New York Times* 9 March (1992): sec. A, col. 3, p. 17.

Kaplan, Harold I., Benjamin J. Sadock, and Jack A. Grebb. *Synopsis of Psychiatry: Behavioral Sciences, Clinical Psychiatry.* Ed. David C. Retford. 7th ed. Baltimore: Williams, 1994.

Kluger, Jeffrey. "Medicating Young Minds." *TIME* magazine 3 November (2003): 48-58.

Kramer, Peter D. "The Transformation of Personality." *Psychology Today* July/August (1993): 42+

Strong, James. *Strong's Exhaustive Concordance of the Bible.*

Toufexis, Anastasia. "The Personality Pill." *TIME* magazine 11 October (1993): 61-62.

Windham, Christopher, and Barbara Martinez. "Article About Antidepressant Stokes Debate on Transparency." *Wall Street Journal* 21 June. (2004): B5.